Waterway Holidays in Britain

This book is about how the average family can have an enjoyable waterway holiday in Britain and Ireland. I shall show you that you do not have to be really energetic or make great physical demands on yourself or your family to enjoy a boating holiday. Not for nothing does one of the holiday agencies publish *A Lazy Man's Guide to Holidays Afloat* every year! More important, you don't have to be an expert sailor or know a great deal about the theories and practices of seamanship.

A waterways holiday in Britain can offer a wide variety of interests and activities and plenty of entertainment on board and on shore, not necessarily very far from home and not too expensively.

Whatever it costs you, your waterway holiday should bring you considerable pleasure. It is not just that you are free on your own boat, nor is it simply the extraordinary peacefulness or great friendliness of everyone you will meet. It is also the feeling that you are about to discover something totally unexpected around the next bend – a castle, windmill, fields of unspoilt countryside, swans and their fluffy cygnets and many more wonderful aspects of nature.

Boulters Lock on the Thames on an August Bank Holiday in the 1890s. See page 90 for an up-to-date comparison.

JANICE ANDERSON

Waterway Holidays in Britain

A "Wish You Were Here" guide

THAMES · MAGNUM

A Thames/Magnum Book

WATERWAY HOLIDAYS IN BRITAIN
0 423 00010 1

First published in Great Britain 1981
by Thames Television in association with Magnum Books

Copyright © 1981 by Janice Anderson

Thames/Magnum Books are published
by Methuen Paperbacks Ltd
11 New Fetter Lane, London EC4P 4EE
in association with Thames Television
International Ltd, 149 Tottenham
Court Road, London WIP 9LL

Photoset in 11pt Garamond by
Robcroft Ltd, London WC1
Made and printed in Great Britain
by Richard Clay (The Chaucer Press) Ltd
Bungay, Suffolk

Contents

Introduction

People in Britain for generations have been attracted to holidays in which water plays a big part in the fun of it all. We are lucky, of course, in the fact that the United Kingdom has an enormous variety of waters for holidaying on: quiet streams, busy rivers, canals, lakes and broads, thousands of miles of indented coastline providing many sheltered bays, inlets and mooring places, and many lovely offshore islands set in waters inviting exploration by yacht and cruiser.

We first took to the seaside in George III's reign and have been going there in great numbers ever since. The Norfolk Broads have been attracting boating holiday-makers since late Victorian times. There was a booking agent at St Olaves in 1890 and Blakes, who are still one of the country's biggest boat holiday agencies, began there in 1902. The River Thames had been giving boating enthusiasts splendid holidays well before Jerome K. Jerome immortalised its Victorian delights in *Three Men in a Boat* in 1889. Sailing and yachting, once the preserve of the well-off, have become more accessible as the designers bring small, inexpensive dinghies and GRP (glass-reinforced plastic) cruisers off their drawing boards and into the boatyards. Local councils the length of the country, seeing the revenue potential, build marinas, tidy up old jetties and landing places, and make sure we have safe moorings for our craft.

For most of us, however – for mum, dad and the kids, and the grandparents as well – the really big step forward in waterway holidays in Britain in the past fifteen years or so has been on Britain's inland waterways, particularly on the narrow canals. Once built to transport goods – coal, grain, clay and china – cheaply and easily in the days before railways and paved roads, these canals have been rescued from neglect and decay by enthusiastic volunteers, local councils and national organisations like the British Waterways Board and the Inland Waterways Association.

The British Waterways Board was established in 1962 by an Act of Parliament to take over the waterways responsibilities of the British Transport Commission, and today the Board own or manage some 2000 miles of inland waterways, from Inverness in Scotland down to Somerset in South West England. About 340 miles of the Board's waterways are available, mainly for commercial usage, but the major part of the system is open to leisure cruising. Add to this the stretches of canal owned by other bodies including the National Trust, plus great river systems like the Thames and the Severn, the Broads and the Fens, and you have a splendid network of nearly 3000 miles of inland waterways which you could explore every summer holiday for years ahead without coming to the end of its potential. And you would be on the safest waterways of any in Europe, largely because there is very little, if any, commercial traffic on large stretches of them. Most canals are also very narrow and not very deep; they should have a 4ft 6in depth of water and, in practice, they generally have about 5ft.

This book is about how the average family can have an enjoyable waterway holiday in Britain and Ireland. I shall show you that you do not have to be really energetic or make great physical demands on yourself or your family to enjoy a boating holiday. Not for nothing does one of the holiday agencies publish *A Lazy Man's Guide to Holidays Afloat* every year! More important, you don't have to be an expert sailor or know a great deal about the theories and practices of seamanship.

I do not go into the question of sailing and yachting holidays very much in this book simply because you can't become a sailing boat skipper in coastal waters or the open sea until you can not only handle a sailing craft but also know something about navigation and seamanship – which cannot be learnt in a short trip out of a marina or boatyard. Of course, you *can* have really energetic, physically demanding holidays on water in Britain if you want to, as *Outdoor and Activity Holidays in Britain* in the same Thames/ Magnum Publications series as this, tells you.

In fact, a waterway holiday in Britain can offer a wide variety of interests and activities and plenty of entertainment on board and on shore, not necessarily very far from home and not too expensively. Even allowing for inflation, a week's waterway holiday in Britain in 1981 need not cost one person much more than £100 in all at the height of the season in July/August, though if you go for the biggest and most luxurious boats with expensive, three-course meals at every stop, the holiday will cost more, of course. You may save up to 50% of the boat hire by taking your holiday early or late in the year – April/May or September/October.

Whatever it costs you, your waterway holiday should bring you considerable pleasure. It is not just that you are free on your own boat to choose your own routes, to decide for yourself when you want to stop for lunch or tea rather than having a coach-driver, airline stewardess or hotel deciding for you. Nor is it simply the extraordinary peacefulness of the whole thing, the wonderful sense of unwinding and loosening of tension you will experience as you glide along in a world where the fastest thing around is likely to be a moorhen scurrying amongst the reeds at the water's edge or a cow munching away in a field. Nor is it the great friendliness you will encounter among people you meet almost anywhere on the inland waterways system, though everyone does seem to have time to say hello and to offer advice if needed, or just to wave as they pass by.

It is also, perhaps most important of all, the feeling that you are always about to discover something totally unexpected round the next bend. It may be just a new

9

view of a familiar building, or an unusual church, castle or windmill, or perhaps just fields of unspoilt countryside in the midst of what you had always thought of as industrial wasteland. For me it is the sight of the great tower of Ely Cathedral, floating hazily on the horizon across the Fens and growing gradually larger as I travel up the Great Ouse, that remains indelibly imprinted on my memory long after everything else. For you, it may be your first Norfolk windmill, or the vast bulk of Windsor Castle looming over the Thames, the rather alarming staircase lock at Bingley, or the toe-curling drop over the side of the Pontcysyllte aqueduct on the Llangollen Canal. Maybe it will just be a pair of swans and their brood of fluffy grey cygnets: if you or your children have never seen them before, they will seem miraculous enough.

The Reculvers.

CHAPTER 1

All About Waterway Holidays

How The Inland Waterway System Developed

As is only to be expected in a country with a long and incident-packed past, Britain's waterway system is choc-a-bloc with historical associations, and just about everywhere you visit will have some interesting story connected with it. Much of the system is man-made and the stories of their building can be fascinating to track down. All the Broads, except Breydon Water at Great Yarmouth which is a natural estuary, resulted from the labours of men; they were medieval peat diggings which were flooded in the fourteenth century and have remained so, for the most part, ever since. Nelson, who was born at Burnham Thorpe in northern Norfolk, had his early introduction to seafaring in Broadland, so every novice having trouble with his sails or trying to push his cruiser off a bank, can take heart from the thought that his lessons are part of a proud tradition.

The Romans dug the first canal in England, the Foss Dyke, from Lincoln to the Trent, which it enters at Torksey. You can still cruise its broad, eleven-mile length, perhaps sparing a thought for the grain boats the Romans sent along it, though they built it and the Caer Dyke, traces of which can still be found on the western edge of the Fens, mainly as drainage works.

After the Romans left Britain, no more canals were made until Elizabeth I's reign. The inhabitants of the country and its invaders made what use they could of existing rivers. In medieval times, some work was done to make river navigation possible further upstream. Weirs and dams were built across rivers to provide enough water

11

A typical canal scene: a narrow boat passing through a bridge. Note the towpath on the left of the picture

power for river-side mills, and flash locks allowed barges to pass through the weirs. By the late Middle Ages, the Severn was one of the busiest navigation rivers in Europe and the rivers of the Fens carried a large cargo traffic.

No-one knows who invented the pound lock, so called because water was 'impounded' between the two sets of doors or gates, though Leonardo da Vinci is said to have built some near Milan in the 1480s. Nor does anyone know who built the first pound lock in Britain though it was very likely John Trew, who built the Exeter Ship Canal, the first real canal to be built in Britain after the Romans. Finished in 1566, the Exeter Ship Canal, which was adapted from an inlet of the Exe river estuary, had three pound locks. It is still used to-day.

Not long after this the first towpath appeared on the River Severn, and tolls for its use were laid down by an Act of Parliament. Towing was done by men, not by the horses, donkeys or mules which were the accepted motive power on the canals till the steam engine took over in the nineteenth century.

The canal system in Britain was very much a private enterprise. The Government did not build canals, although no canal could be dug without an Act of Parliament being passed first. By the early eighteenth century many rivers up and down the country had been made navigable over long stretches, allowing many thousands of tons of cargo to pass over the country at a pace and cost which would have been impossible by packhorse or existing roads. Up to the middle of the eighteenth century, most Acts were to allow people to scour out river beds and improve existing navigations rather than build completely new ones. Such Acts gave the builders powers to buy up land, dig the canal and exact tolls from its users. They also obliged owners to keep their waterways in good repair, and to allow any craft who wanted to use them to do so, provided they were of a suitable size. Then Francis, 3rd Duke of Bridgewater, appeared on the scene.

Bridgewater had seen canals being used in France and the Low Countries and conceived the idea of building a canal of his own to carry coal from his mines near Worsley to Manchester. His was not the very first of the eighteenth-century canals in England, the honour of which must go to the Sankey Brook Canal from St Helens to the Mersey, (another canal was the Newry canal in Northern Ireland, opened in 1745), but it was the Bridgewater Navigation, as it came to be called, which really opened people's eyes to the enormous potential of water as a cheap, efficient means of transport in an age when most roads were poorly maintained and often impassable in bad weather, and when no-one had seen the transport potential of the new steam power. It was the canal system linking up the four great river systems in England (the Thames, Severn, Mersey and Trent) which allowed the Industrial and the Agricultural Revolutions in Britain to take their first big strides.

The Act which permitted the duke to 'make a navigable Cut or Canal from a certain place in the township of Salford, to or near Worsley Mill and Middlewood in the manor of Worsley' provided he observe certain restrictions against the pulling down of houses and the cutting down of trees, was passed in 1759 and the canal was begun at once. The story of its digging is vividly recounted in *The Story of Our Inland Waterways* by Robert Aikman. It is now out of print but can be found in many public libraries.

The duke and his brilliant engineer, James Brindley, had many difficulties to contend with, not the least of which was financial. The duke had planned to build his canal only as far as Barton in the Irwell Valley, whence his boats would descend to the Irwell via a lock and then use the river into Manchester. The Mersey and Irwell Navigation Company, seeing a way to make a fine profit, indicated that they would charge the duke the highest toll possible to transport his coal on their river, three shillings and fourpence a ton.

'Right,' said Brindley, 'we'll build an aqueduct over the Irwell and take our canal all the way into Manchester.'

The Navigation Company, seeing their fat profit disappearing, offered a new toll, sixpence a ton. But Bridgewater went back to Parliament, obtained a new act allowing him to build a longer canal with an aqueduct, and carried on. His canal was opened in 1761, and the duke's coal reached Manchester so inexpensively that the price in the town was reduced from sevenpence to threepence a hundredweight. At the time, the duke was nearly ruined financially – the total cost of the Bridgewater Navigation was £300,000, a huge sum in those days – but later his canal made him so rich that people spoke with awe of the 'Bridgewater Millions'.

Brindley's Barton Aqueduct was 200 yards long and rose 39 feet above the river Irwell at its highest point. The arch through which boats could sail underneath was 63 feet wide, and people, forgetting that the Romans had used aqueducts to carry water for miles, were amazed that no water dropped from the canal so far above their heads. It stood until 1893 when, because it was not high enough to allow full-size sailing vessels to pass underneath, it had to be demolished as part of the work which converted the Irwell into a section of the Manchester Ship Canal. Its replacement was that great wonder of the canal system, the Barton Swing Aqueduct which, when its ends were sealed off by gates, swings open to allow ships to pass through on the Ship Canal beneath. You are not allowed to leave your boat in the 'tank' as it swings open and shut again, so if you are ever held up there waiting to cross, take time to remember the Duke of Bridgewater and his clever engineer who began the whole waterway system on which you have been travelling.

In the seventy years or so following the opening of the Bridgewater Canal, the extent of navigable inland waterways in Britain grew from about 1500 miles to more than 5000. Some of this increase was due to a more efficient use being made of river navigation, but the greatest extension came from the building of canals. Britain experienced a real canal mania early in the 1790s when public companies set up to build canals had their shares fully subscribed by eager buyers long before their enabling Act had made its way through Parliament. One such subscriber was Josiah Wedgwood, the great pottery maker, who contributed large sums to the building of the Trent and Mersey Canal. Two Wedgwood factories, at Etruria and Barleston, were on the canal, and they use it to this day to transport china clay from Cornwall via the Mersey to their works. Transportation by water was also much kinder to the finished china than the eighteenth century road transport would have been, as Josiah was quick to see.

If the profits to be gained from canal tolls were vast, then so too were the costs involved in building canals, and not all of them were financially successful. Some encountered unforeseen engineering problems or did not take sufficient account of the need to ensure a good supply of water to the canal, and others found it difficult to obtain building materials or hire sufficient labour. The canals, like the railways of the nineteenth century, were built more or less by hand by armies of labourers, called 'navigators' or 'navvies', many of whom were little more than unruly, drunken mobs. Some canals were built too late in the period and ran into stiff competition from the new railways before they could earn back their capital outlay.

It was, in fact, James Brindley's fault that the canal system as a whole was unable to offer much resistance to the railways. Partly for reasons of economy, and partly to use less water which was not always easy to collect and store, Brindley abandoned the broad measure he had used in the Bridgewater Canal and decided on a width of only seven feet for the locks of his later canals.

Other engineers saw that Brindley's canal dimensions could prove uneconomic and many canals were built with locks wide enough to take barges with a fourteen-foot beam, most notably the Leeds and Liverpool, the Lancaster, the Kennet and Avon, the Rochdale, the Grand Junction and the Forth and Clyde. But too many of Brindley's canals, which included the Staffordshire and Worcestershire, the Birmingham, the Coventry and the Oxford, ran through what were to become key industrial

16

areas, and narrow boats carrying a maximum load of thirty tons just could not compete with the steam railway.

So, by the middle of Queen Victoria's reign, the great canal boom was over. This is not to say that the system fell into disuse completely. Far from it. We have already mentioned the building of the Manchester Ship Canal, which opened for business in 1894, and the New Junction Canal which was built in 1905. Many canals continued to do commercial business up to World War II, but it was local rather than national business, and by the war's end tonnage carried on canals was a third of what it had been at the beginning of the century.

After the war, the government brought some 60% of the remaining waterways within the orbit of the British Transport Commission. The main waterways remaining outside this nationalisation were the River Thames, the East Anglia rivers and waterways (the Broads), the Great Ouse and the Nene systems in the Fens, the Manchester Ship Canal, the Bridgewater Canal, the Rochdale Canal, and various other small rivers and canals. Under the Transport Act of 1947 the nationalised waterways were put in the control of the Commission's Docks and Inland Waterways Executive, which laid the groundwork for planning a future for them. The future became more rosy when a special British Waterways Board was established by an Act of Parliament in 1962 to take over the Commission's responsibility for the inland waterways and has looked promising since the Board was given a perm-anent 'charter' in the Transport Act of 1968. This Act required the Board to make 340 miles of the waterways in their care available mainly for commercial carriage of freight, and 1100 miles for recreational purposes. The remainder have also come to be used largely for leisure activities.

The Board, working in co-operation and harmony with local bodies and guided and influenced by canal preser-vation societies, most notably the Inland Waterways Association, has brought hundreds of miles of near-derelict, unused canals back to life again. In a remarkably short space of time we have been given a whole new leisure world – a 'linear national park' 2000 miles long.

In fact, we should all be grateful to Mr Brindley for his miscalculation. It has meant that we now possess a leisure-time waterway system unique in Europe in that most of it is quite free of commercial traffic; we have it to ourselves to cruise about in, fish on, bird-watch from, walk along the tow-paths, or just quietly do nothing in.

Business Is Booming

The boat hire agencies, who have done their market research, tell us that one out of every two people in Britain is interested in boats and boating. It seems, in fact, that half the population agrees with the famous remark of the Water Rat in *The Wind in the Willows*: 'Believe me, my young friend, there is *nothing* – absolutely nothing – half so much worth doing as simply messing about in boats.'

Many people, of course, own their own boats, and for them a boat is much more than just a holiday object. But for most people wanting a waterway holiday, hiring a boat is the best answer; they don't want to sink a lot of capital into a boat they may only use a couple of times a year, and they do not want to be involved in all the problems of repair and maintenance. More than half a million people take a hire-boat holiday in Britain every year and the growth rate in recent years has been estimated at about 10% per annum, though it is recognised that this increase may slow slightly as the capacity of Britain's waterways is not limitless. Though they have not been able to greatly increase the amount of inland waterways available to them, boat hire companies have been able to expand their capacity in two other ways; by building larger and more luxurious boats which can sleep up to twelve people, and by extending the length of the season. Back in 1890, the first hire-boat people had only about seven or eight weeks of the year in which they could make their profits. Today's hire companies can reckon on at least twenty-five weeks for the majority of their boats, with a few being kept in operation for most of the year. Winter holidays have become more attractive as boats have been fitted with good heating systems; about a quarter of all hire boats now have central heating, and the rest have some form of other heating.

Boats, in fact, have become generally a lot more sophisticated in recent years, and heating, refrigerators, showers and flush toilets have become the rule rather than the exception. According to Mr James Hoseason, Managing Director of Hoseasons Holidays, Great Britain can boast of having more live-aboard cabin hire craft on its waterways than the rest of the Western world put together.

The greatest amount of hire-boat holiday business is still done on the Norfolk Broads, which accounts for not far short of 50% of the market in Britain. In 1979, the latest year for which figures are available, there were nearly 2300 boats – mostly yachts and cruisers – for holiday hire on the Broads. Britain's canals, where business did not really get going until the 1960s, could offer over 1600 hire-boats, over 80% of them modern, recently built craft. The Thames, where private boat ownership is much greater than on the canals, came third in the league, with Scotland fourth and the Fenlands fifth. There is comparatively little holiday hire-boat business in the Lake District, not because the Lakes are not immensely attractive, but because individually they are too small to make a cruising holiday a worthwhile proposition. You could get from one end of Ullswater to the other in a couple of hours in any case.

The hire-boat companies can also say, with justification, that if business has been good for them in recent years, it has also been good for the towns and villages on the waterway banks. Holiday boat people bring them business not just in the recognised peak time of July and August but in the 'shoulder months' of March, April, May, September and October as well – a much longer season than most seaside resorts can expect – and it is a pleasant business; quiet boats don't belch petrol fumes and jam up roadways, and the boats' occupants usually come into town with their shopping bags ready to spend quite a bit of cash. According to Mr David Court of Blakes Holidays, boat hiring holidaymakers in mainland Britain spent an average of £160,000 a day for seven months of the year in 1979. 'And that,' said Mr Court, 'ain't hay.'

The boat hire people are also looking at ways of extending their business into new parts of the country. The first hire base on Loch Lomond in Scotland was opened in 1980 and boat hire bases are also appearing on the lochs and estuaries of the Western Highlands. This is taking the companies and their customers into the business of sea cruising, which the former sees as a natural progression from canal and river cruising, though it is rather more adventurous and expensive, and requires a bit more experience than is necessary on inland waterways.

British boat hirers have also moved over the Channel into Northern France and the Low Countries, which is a story outside the scope of this book, though it is perhaps worth noting that many of the boats used today by French and German operators were built in Britain, the British having been in the business for much longer and in a much bigger way so that they are aware of what their customers want.

The Kinds of Boats Available

The range of holiday hire-boats available is impressive and your choice will depend very much on where you want to go, how much you yourself want to be involved in the sailing of the boat, and, of course, how much you want to spend on the holiday.

Before you make the final decision, try and visit one or two boatyards and have a look over the different kinds of boat. The boat companies are generally very pleased to have you taking an interest in their craft. Try not to turn up in the middle of their change-over day in July or

Holiday craft on the Thames above Shiplake lock

One of the pleasures of a canal holiday: a waterside pub

August, as they have a lengthy check list to go through with each boat in the few hours between one party leaving and another coming aboard.

At the quieter ends of the season some self-drive hire companies make their boats available for short and weekend hire. This is a good opportunity to find out if you are going to like them for a longer holiday.

The Earls Court Boat Show in London every January is also a good place to see holiday boats at close quarters.

Whatever the craft you finally decide on you can be assured that it will conform to a professional standard of safety and maintenance. Organisations like Blakes, the hire-boat agency which is owned by its member operators, Hoseasons, other booking agencies and the Association of Pleasure Craft Operators have their own high standards which boats within their organisations must adhere to. The British Waterways Board also has stringent building and safety regulations with which all boats must comply to get a licence allowing them to operate on the Board's waterways.

Motor Cruiser

There are more cruisers than any other kind of boat on Britain's inland waterways, most of them very modern in design and function, with GRP hulls and accommodating from two to twelve people. Some cruisers have the sleek hulls of yachts, others the broad-beamed shape of barges. Wide-beam cruisers are generally more roomy inside than narrow boats or the small cruisers that will fit into narrow canal locks. A really big, 44-foot cruiser with a 12-foot beam may even run to a bath below deck, though boats this size will not be seen on many parts of the canal system, of course: the Broads and the Thames are their happy hunting grounds.

At the other end of the size scale, a small 20-foot cruiser can offer two or three people a holiday with more than adequate comforts: refrigerator, shower, heating and flush toilet are all available on many small cruisers. If you are very tall, the main problems with these are likely to be the headroom below deck which may only be 5ft 6in, and the length of the berths which may not quite make the 6 foot minimum which the boat companies generally set themselves.

Although petrol engines have been replaced by diesel on most cruisers, you will still find the former on some small ones, and this is another point to watch out for, as finding somewhere to buy petrol in remote parts can be a problem – though it can add to the fun of the holiday, too, and give a tale to tell back home. Running out of fuel is not usually a problem with diesel engines as the boat can hold sufficient to last the whole trip.

Most diesel engines are operated by a simple gear stick-push forward to move forward, pull back to reverse. Steering on motor cruisers is generally a wheel rather than a tiller, and may be situated fore, aft or in the centre.

Whatever its size, and the position of its steering, the motor cruiser is easy to manoeuvre, and you do not have to be a car driver to cope. In fact car drivers, used to the instant response of brake, clutch and accelerator, may take a little while to get used to the delayed reaction of the boat's equivalents. Not that boats have an equivalent of the car's brakes: you put the engine into reverse to slow and stop, so you have to learn to anticipate when you are going to slow down.

Finally, a point about the electricity available on cruisers. It is generated from the battery and provides lighting, shaver and television points. It cannot be used to power other electric appliances. So your own pop-up toaster, coffee percolator, electric hair rollers etc. will have to stay at home.

The Narrow Boat

This is the traditional boat of the narrow canal and is never more than 6ft 10in wide. The waterway historian,

Charles Hadfield, says that the boat was probably developed from the small mine boats which were used in the workings of the Duke of Bridgewater's coalmines at Worsley, and which James Brindley must have seen at work. The narrow boat itself was designed to fit the seven-foot narrow locks of James Brindley's canals. Originally pulled along the towpaths by horse or mule, the boats came to be powered by steam engines. Today's pleasure narrow boats are almost always powered by diesel.

Even in their early days, when they were mostly used for transporting freight, canal boats called 'fly-boats' carried passengers in quite large numbers and could be much quicker and more reliable than the cumbersome stage coach. Until the coming of the railways they were an important form of passenger transport, especially in places remote from good toll roads.

The narrow boat you choose today is likely to have been built within the past ten years – or even last winter, for the boat companies regularly put new boats in their fleets. It will probably have a steel hull, as this is much easier to repair and maintain than wood. Of the few old wooden-hulled narrow boats left, most are in the careful and loving ownership of private enthusiasts or societies.

Outside you will notice that the narrow boat steers by a tiller from an open well in the stern, and that it is perhaps not so gaily painted and decorated with castles and roses as you may romantically have supposed. Again, this is a matter of upkeep: the boat companies cannot spend a lot of time maintaining the sparkling condition of an ornately decorated boat. On the other hand, most companies have devised for their boats an attractive livery in distinctive colours, often including some decorative elements. You may find the traditional narrow boat decoration turning up on waste-bins, buckets or teapots. Unlike most cruisers, narrow boats don't have protection from bad weather, so the person standing in the stern well steering would be well advised to have a rain-proof anorak.

Inside, today's narrow boat is nothing like the tiny

cramped cabins fore and aft of the main hold with which narrow boat families of days gone by had to make do. The interior of your boat will have been designed with every modern comfort in mind, including television. Showers, flush toilets, full sized gas cookers, refrigerators, space or central heating, even duvets on the berths, are more or less standard equipment. Like cruisers, however, a narrow boat's electrical system will not take any domestic electrical appliances.

The smallest narrow boat, of which there are not too many available for hire, is about 28 feet long, and sleeps three or four people; the largest may be 70 feet long and sleep twelve people. Most narrow boats come within the 40 to 60 foot range and sleep six to eight people.

The Hotel Boat

This is the luxury end of the hire-boat business: just bring your toothbrush and a few casual clothes, sit back and enjoy it all, including excellent food cooked often to *cordon bleu* standards. A hotel boat may be one large cruiser sleeping about ten people and cruising through Broadland, or it may be two 70-foot narrow boats sleeping up to twelve and with many miles of the Midlands canal network at its disposal. On either, the passengers may do as little or as much as they choose. The boats have full-time crews, who work the boats and do the cooking; they also have comfortable lounges, well-stocked bars and small libraries. The private cabins are single or two-berth, and are therefore ideal for people on their own, or for couples who do not want to hire a boat just for the two of them. There is no route planning to be done as this is all worked out in advance by the boat's owners or crew; there is no work to be done either, unless the passengers would like to help get the boat through a lock, and there are plenty of stopping places en route. Passengers can even take a constitutional by walking along the towpath to the next bridge or lock – and they will probably need some exercise, if only to walk off all the food. All hotel boat brochures emphasise the food angle – early morning tea in bed, hearty English breakfast, morning coffee, lunch, afternoon tea and cakes, dinner . . . phew!

A point to remember about hotel boats is that they often cruise a one-way route; that is, they do not necessarily end their trip at the base they started from. This is why operators suggest that their clients arrive by public transport; if they come by car, they may find themselves at the end of their trip miles from where they left their car. Hotel boat bases are generally within easy reach of a railway station.

A variation on the hotel boat theme is the private hotel boat, which may be chartered by one group of people. The boat is fully crewed and all your meals are prepared for you.

A hotel boat holiday is, not surprisingly, more expensive per person than a self-drive hire boat holiday, and about half the hotel boats do not take children under twelve or fourteen years.

Sailing Craft

A sailing boat obviously requires more knowledge and expertise to handle than cruisers or narrow boats. The sailor has to be much more aware of wind and water conditions and to understand something of how his boat will react in those conditions. This is not to say that a complete beginner could not take out a sailing boat. With help he could, though he would be most unwise to do so in coastal waters or out at sea.

This is one reason why sailing boat holiday hire in Britain is concentrated so much on the Norfolk Broads. These are reasonably safe waters on which to take a family sailing. Both Blakes and Hoseasons can arrange sailing tuition for beginners on the Broads, and retain certain boatyards to do this work. They reckon that three hours' tuition with an experienced yachtsman is about all most people need to make them competent enough to take a sailing boat on the protected waters of the Broads.

The long-established boatyard of Herbert Woods at Potter Heigham provides tuition for Blakes' customers and has had would-be sailors who have known absolutely nothing about boats and sailing and who have coped reasonably well after three hours' tuition. In fact, though, they have found that most people have had some experience of dinghy sailing or have, at the very least, read a book or two before turning up, so that they do know the difference between a halyard and a sheet, in theory at least.

An average tuition course will introduce the novice to all parts of the boat, explaining the functions of the different sails and ropes and giving practical demonstrations, in which the learner takes part, of such essentials as mooring head to wind, to hoist or lower sail, how to reef, and how to come on to a mooring. The learner will practise under supervision everything he needs to know to handle a boat safely in the close Broad waters.

Another hire-boat sailing area is off the west coast of Scotland, and here novices are asked to sail in specified safe waters – the northern end of Loch Fyne is one. More experienced sailors may take hire yachts further, around the sea lochs and estuaries, or they may join specially arranged small flotillas in which the mother ship has a very experienced skipper and the smaller yachts are expected to have at least one experienced person on board. These flotilla holidays are available in Scotland and down on England's south coast.

For everyone there is a good variety of sailing craft available for hire. They range in size from 21-footers, sleeping two, up to about 34 feet with berths for up to seven. Most are Bermuda or Gaff rigged, the traditional Broads rig, and are easier to handle than the larger offshore boats. Sailing craft include cruisers, which have engines as well as sails, and yachts which come with sails only but to which outboard engines can be fitted for an extra fee.

Most sailing craft have much the same basics as motor cruisers and narrow boats: gas cookers, some form of food cold-storage (though not necessarily a refrigerator), full-length berths (which usually mean 6 feet long), electric light, flush toilet, and cold water storage. Many do not have running hot water and most do not have heating.

Sailing Barge

Most of the lovely old red-sailed barges which were once such a familiar sight round the Thames Estuary and the south-east coast of England have disappeared. A few are still working, some as floating hotels, on which fully catered sailing holidays can be enjoyed by groups of up to twelve passengers whose two- and three-berth cabins have been built in the former cargo hold. With their 18–20 foot beams, these barges are quite spacious, with roomy saloon and cabins, and even a bath among the toilet facilities.

This is undoubtedly a more exciting kind of holiday: you are at sea with 3500 square feet of sail above you and an appetite-sharpening breeze about you. The crew will be happy to have you help pull on ropes or weigh anchor if you want to, but there is no need for you to do so if you would rather just relax on deck. Because the Thames barge has a comparatively shallow draft it can sail up rivers, estuaries and creeks, which adds to the variety of scenery to be encountered.

One company, Anglian Yacht Services, has a programme of specialist birdwatching and art cruises as well as their general holiday cruises (see Chapter 3, The Boat Hire Companies, for details). Anglian also emphasise that you do not have to be young and fit to enjoy a holiday on a sailing barge; one of their customers was an eighty-nine-year-old lady who had broken her arm the week before her holiday began and she thoroughly enjoyed herself on board.

Camping Boats

These are probably best left to the young and fit or to those who don't mind roughing it a bit. A camping boat holiday gives you a good opportunity to experience a narrow boat as it was before twentieth century soft-living caught up with it, for the sleeping accommodation is basically the hold with a canvas cover.

These camping boats are popular with youth groups and school parties and are comparatively inexpensive. Boats may be hired with a crew, or self-driven, and hirers usually have to bring their own bedding and sometimes their own crockery and cutlery.

Canoes

Inland and coastal canoeing in Britain uses both kayaks and Canadian-style canoes and can be exciting and dangerous. White-water kayak canoeing is for the experts but there is quieter canoe camping for groups of people. You do not have to be young to enjoy a canoeing holiday – I know a married couple (who would agree that they are middle-aged) who spent a summer two years ago paddling a large Canadian canoe down the Danube from its source to the mouth – but you do have to be reasonably fit. An article in a recent issue of *Canoeing Magazine* said that anyone contemplating a canoe trip up the Kennet and Avon Canal should train by running round assault courses with a boat on their shoulder!

Canoe camping using craft light enough to be portered around obstacles such as disused locks, can take you into waterways where no cruiser or narrowboat can penetrate. Kathleen Tootill, the well-known British canoeist, suggests in *Canoeing Complete* that the best boat for inland touring by canoe in Britain on not too difficult waters would have a length of about 14 feet, a 24-26 inch beam, and a slightly rockered bottom.

The Barge.

CHAPTER 2

Planning a Holiday

How To Go About It

Planning a summer boating holiday is an ideal occupation for a winter's Sunday afternoon. There you are on the sitting room floor, brochures and maps spread out all round you, conjuring up visions of pleasant summer days with blue skies and a few cotton-wool clouds floating above you, the gentle lap of water beneath you, green trees and quiet fields all round you while you build up a splendid tan.

Romantic perhaps, but realistic too. The hire companies and the booking agencies have their brochures and prices ready in the November before the season starts, and the agencies have their telephones manned seven days a week in January, February and March to deal with bookings. Thus, in order to have the widest possible choice of boats and dates at your disposal, particularly if you must take your holiday during the school summer holidays, you should start thinking about it before Christmas.

Getting The Facts

Your local travel agent may stock the brochures of the five main agents. If not, write direct or telephone them. (Addresses and phone numbers are listed in Chapter 3, pages 50-59.) You will usually receive the brochures within three or four days of asking.

There are as many as two hundred hire-boat companies (which is why I do not have room to list them all in this book!) and many of them do not hire out their boats through the big agencies. You can find out who they are and what they offer from several publications: *THE CANAL BOOK, THE THAMES BOOK* and *THE BROADS BOOK*, all published by Link House Publications; *INLAND WATERWAYS GUIDE* published by the Inland Waterways Association; and *THE WATERWAY USERS COMPANION* put out by the British Waterways Board. Details of where to obtain these are in the second section of this chapter, Books and Other Publications, p 40, which also tells you about maps and route planners.

Deciding Where To Go

We hope that the section in Chapter 1 describing the different kinds of hire-boats available will have helped you decide which one is right for you. If so, then your choice of where to go is partly made for you; if you have decided on a wide-beam cruiser then you are probably thinking of the Broads, the Thames or Loch Ness and the Caledonian Canal. If you have set your heart on a narrow boat then the English and Welsh canal network is at your disposal.

Having decided on your area, you can pin-point your starting place more precisely. If you have to rely on public transport, for instance, you will not want to choose a boatyard too far from a railway station or bus depot. Nor will you want to choose one too far from the part of the country you want to explore: boating is not a speedy activity and a boatyard thirty miles away from where you want to be is, in fact, two solid cruising days away.

Do not make the mistake of hiring a broad-beam boat on a wide canal when you also want to explore some narrow canals. On the other hand, some of the broad canals – the Leeds and Liverpool for instance – have short locks which will not take a 70-foot narrow boat, so this is another point to bear in mind.

Don't be over-ambitious; planning a trip which requires you to travel twenty miles a day would mean cutting out all stops or travelling after dark, which is something you will almost certainly not be allowed to do under the terms of the hire agreement. The hire companies do not equip their boats with the lights needed and you would not be insured against accident if you travelled at night.

This may sound complicated, but don't worry. If you tell the booking agency or hire company exactly what your plans are, they will alert you to any likely problems and even suggest alternative yards or routes. This is another good reason for doing some advance planning as it ensures that you arrive at your chosen boatyard to step aboard the best boat for you, with the correct licences, and in the general area you want to cruise in.

Choosing Your Hire Company

The choice of hire company should be made on the basis of your own requirements and you should not need to ask questions about the general state of the boats. You can assume that they are seaworthy, their engines have been properly maintained, their fuel safely stored or their sails all in order, partly because there are several boards and associations whose job it is to ensure that these things are done, and partly because it is not in the hirers' interest for their boats to be anything less than sound – they want your custom again. It is wise to make a short list of, say, five or six companies which meet your requirements so that you have alternatives ready should your first choice be fully booked.

Points you should note as you look through the brochures and catalogues include:

Will the waterway you have in mind give you the sort of holiday you want? If you are after a quiet holiday in the countryside, really away from it all, including other people, then you do not want to choose a canal or canals which will take you through much built-up or industrial country; nor do you want a really popular canal like the Llangollen where you may find yourself joining queues to get through locks (which is a reason for avoiding the Thames as well in July and August), and maybe even the very popular Broads will be too crowded for you in July and August. On the other hand, if you want a holiday where you can leave the boat several times a day to visit somewhere interesting, then the Broads could be just the area for you, as could the Thames with its many historic towns, royal associations and famous riverside pubs, or some of the Midlands canals which have towns, stately homes and battlefields a short distance from the waterway.

Is the start day of the hire company you have in mind convenient for you? The 'start day' is the day of the week on which the hire company has its boats ready for new parties to take them over. Most companies' start days are at weekends, but a few do have mid-week starts which may be more convenient for people who have to work at weekends. Don't forget to note the finish time, too. For boats hired, say, on a Saturday afternoon, the return-to-base time is usually early or mid-morning the following Saturday (for a week's hire), but some companies ask for the boats to be returned on the Friday evening.

Do the hire fees quoted in the brochures include everything? Some apparently low fees may turn out to be as high as anyone else's by the time you have added in the fuel costs, linen hire and television hire that others include in the fee. One cost which you must add to the quoted fees for self-drive boats is Value Added Tax. Hotel boats and sailing barges include VAT in their fees, but self-drive boats do not, and it must be paid at the full current standard rate. The reason companies and agencies do not include it is because the Government is quite likely to change it after their brochures have been printed, and hire costs could be affected if a company's tax point date (and it varies from company to company) gets caught up in the government's tax rate changes. (Hotel boats can include VAT in their fees because their

The well-known canal-side figure, the late Mr Jack James, shows how to make a rope fender at the Waterways Museum, Stoke Bruerne

VAT rate is something they work out individually with their local Customs and Excise office. Deciding their rate is a complicated business depending on finding a neat balance between the amount of catering, accommodation and other facilities on offer from each company.)

Will the boat company allow you to take the boat where you want to go, and have they licensed it to do so? Some companies will not allow their boats to be taken out of the canal system and on to a river, such as the Severn or the Thames. Most Thames companies will not allow you to take their boats below Teddington Lock. Those operating off the west coast of Scotland either will not hire out sailing craft to people without experience or they define limits beyond which novice sailors must not go.

Do the hire companies of your choice allow pets on board their boats? Most do, with the proviso that they must be kept off bedding and seats, but some don't, so it is wise to check. Many also add extra fees for allowing pets on board.

Deciding On A Boat

As with the hire companies, it is sensible not to pin all your holiday plans on just one boat in a brochure, even if its name or shape are the ones you have been dreaming about for as long as you can remember. All boats comply to the same minimum requirements, anyway, and it is the fine detail you should consider with some care.

The minimum standards you can expect to find on all boats whose companies are part of an agency booking scheme, and on most independently operated boats are:

Berths (beds): 6 feet long with interior sprung or foam mattresses. Because berths often double as daytime seating, they may be covered with furnishing quality plastic, which can be awkward to sleep on. The sheets slip off and the beds may get rather hot in summer. If in doubt about comfort, take extra sheets to wrap round the mattresses.

Bed linen: either sheets and blankets, sleeping bags and liner sheets, or duvets, pillows and pillow cases are almost always supplied. But do check. A few companies don't supply them, particularly on camping boats.

When considering a boat's layout, check where the berths are to ensure that the member of the party who insists on a sleeping section to him or herself can get it, or that grandma does not have to climb up into a top bunk. Check that there is room for an infant's cot, or that the hire company can provide berth sides so that a small child will not fall out of bed.

Galleys (kitchens): designed to get as many modern conveniences into as small a space as possible. Narrow boats and cruisers will have Calor gas cookers not much smaller than an ordinary domestic cooker, usually with three or four burners, a grill and an oven. On sailing craft the cooker will often be rather smaller, with only two burners, though it will usually have an oven and grill as well.

If you have never cooked with Calor gas before, you should read carefully the notes which all the agencies include in their handbooks or brochures. Calor gas is safe and simple to use provided you follow a few simple rules. Here they are, adapted from the notes in the agencies' booklets:

Ensure that there is good ventilation in the galley or saloon before you use the cooker (or the gas space heater, too, of course). You don't want a draught, though, as this could blow the burners out.

Light the gas as soon as you turn it on – in fact, light your match first.

Never leave the cooker unattended, so that should a burner blow out you will be there to relight it at once. If you let unburnt gas escape it could collect in the bilges where it could become a very explosive mixture.

Always shut the oven door carefully as slamming it

could blow the burners out. If you think that the oven burner may have gone out, turn off the gas rings above before you open the oven doors.

Unless your refrigerator also works from the main bottle supply it is a good idea to turn the main gas supply off at the cylinder if you are not going to use it for some hours.

Your hire company will usually ensure that you have sufficient gas to last your whole trip, with normal use. The gas cylinders will be stored in a locker which vents overboard. Always use one cylinder until it is empty, then switch over to the other. When you take over your boat remember to ask the boatyard staff to show you where the cylinders are stored, how they shut off, and how you switch from an empty one to a full one.

Most boats have reasonable size working surfaces in the galley and a good selection of pots, pans and other kitchen items, crockery and cutlery. (You will usually receive an inventory among the papers and leaflets the hire company sends you, or you will find one on board, waiting to be checked over, when you arrive.) Cruisers and narrow boats will generally have a refrigerator, operated from the gas cylinder, but some sailing craft may have only an icebox or cold food cabinet.

This seems a good point at which to remind you to check on whether the hire company you are considering is able to arrange for groceries to be delivered to your boat before you set off on your holiday. Many can arrange this service through local shops, at no profit to themselves, but at considerable convenience to you. You just have to send them a list of your requirements in good time and they pass it on to the local store who delivers direct to your boat.

Another reminder when talking about the galley: never, never throw rubbish over board. Cans rust but remain to litter the scene and plastic bags are a real menace, as they can wrap themselves round boat propellers. So remember to have a good supply of rubbish bags on board in which rubbish can be kept until you reach a disposal point.

There are plenty of them along the waterways.

Toilet facilities: well up to domestic standards though, naturally enough, sometimes rather cramped. There won't be room to wave your arms about vigorously while towelling yourself after a shower. Apart from a few smaller yachts, most hire boats today have hot and cold water showers as well as wash basins. N.B. at this point: hire companies do not supply towels, so these must be added to your own inventory of things to take on holiday with you.

Almost all boats now have modern flush toilets, too. Waste-matter is stored aboard in sealed, completely hygienic conditions until it is pumped ashore into special disposal units. On a week's cruise, you probably won't have to worry about emptying; the boatyard staff will take care of this when you get back to base. On a longer cruise, the toilet may have to be flushed out, but there are special pumping out stations all over the waterway system, generally with staff to do the work for you. You have to pay a pump-out fee at the time for this service, and another point to check out in your brochures is whether or not the hire company will reimburse you for this as many do. (There is a list of pump-out stations at the end of the book (pages 189-196).

A couple of don'ts about boat toilets whether of the older chemical kind (and there are not too many of these left) or the more modern, flush, pump-out toilet:

Don't drop things down them and do not try to flush disposable baby nappies, sanitary towels or tampons down them. These must be disposed of ashore.

Don't clean them out with Harpic or other lavatory cleaners, bleaches, disinfectants etc. as these destroy the action of the chemicals in them.

Good supplies of fresh water: All boat companies will tell you that they give you plenty of fresh water, and so they do, bearing in mind that there must be an upper limit to the size of the water tank which you could reasonably expect to find on board a family-size cruiser. But you are not sailing on the *QE2*, and you should not be as profligate with water on a boat as most of us are at home. Don't wash the lettuce under running water, for instance, or leave the water running while you are cleaning your teeth, or stand under the shower for too long. Always make sure when you take over your boat that you know where to fill the water tank (and that you can distinguish the water intake from the fuel intake!) and try to remember to top up every time you see a filling point at a mooring place.

Electricity: generated from the engine battery, lights your boat, powers the television, if any, and powers an electric razor. As we said earlier, it will not operate ordinary domestic appliances like toasters, coffee grinders or electric hair rollers.

The *engines* of most cruisers and narrow boats have an electric start – either by turning a key or pushing a button. Most hire-boat engines these days are diesel which are cheaper to run and require refuelling less often than petrol, but you should check this point as some boats still have petrol engines. Controls are very simple – either a single lever that provides both forward and reverse gear and speed control, or a double lever, one of which controls the gear and the other the throttle.

A final point worth considering is whether to go for a boat which is bigger than your requirements – a five-berth for four people, for instance. If you can afford the larger hire fee it is a good idea as it gives more storage space, always at a premium, and may mean that the dining table can always remain as such without having to be converted into a berth every night.

Books And Other Publications

Inland waterway holidays generate a surprising amount of paper material. There are the brochures and information booklets which the agencies and hire companies send out; the maps, timetables and route planners needed to plan a holiday in advance and to help you get the maximum enjoyment out of it as you go along; and a good selection of annual publications aimed specifically at the holidaymaker and which cover everything from where to hire, moor and eat to things to see and do. There are also the many magazines which the real enthusiast will want to have on a regular basis, including monthlies like *Waterways World, Canal and River Boat, Motor Boat and Yachting, Waterways News, Yachting Monthly* and *Canoeist Magazine*.

There have also been many books written about the waterways, particularly canals, and a delve into a few of these can add to the pleasure to be gained from the holiday. They can alert the reader to a wide variety of things concerned with history, architecture, natural history and so on to look out for as his boat travels along.

Annual Publications

THE BROADS BOOK '81
THE CANAL BOOK '81
THE THAMES BOOK '81
Three softcover books published by Link House Publications Ltd. Planned as all-purpose guides for the holidaymaker, their detailed information includes navigation strip maps and guides, town directories, lists of hire firms, notes on fishing, and some pointers to places to visit and things to do. Each book also contains articles on specific aspects of the subject – restoring and preserving Broadlands windmills, or how to cope with canal locks etc.

THE GOOD BOAT GUIDE 1981 by Bryan Marsh (Penguin Books). A very useful reference guide to boat hire companies operating on rivers and canals. Companies are given a merit rating from one to five, and a value-for-money rating in five categories: excellent, very good, good, satisfactory or poor. Should help to keep the hire companies on their toes – though most of them don't need to be.

INLAND WATERWAYS GUIDE (published jointly by

the Inland Waterways Association and Haymarket Publishing Ltd). This book has maps and guides to 3000 miles of waterways, including the canal system, the Thames, Severn and the Broads, and the rivers and Middle Level Navigations of the Fens. It also has a comprehensive list of boat hire companies with their addresses, areas of operation, and their kind of boats and facilities. Obtainable from newsagents like Smiths, or direct from the IWA, 114 Regents Park Road, London NW1 8UQ.

WHERE TO LAUNCH YOUR BOAT. This one is for the boat owner, rather than the boat hirer, but as the booklet also includes useful facts about boat services, fuel supplies and parking facilities in the vicinity of the mooring sites, all boating holidaymakers will find it useful. It includes nearly 1600 launching sites, on rivers, lakes and broads, canals and the coasts of England, the Isle of Man, the Channel Islands, Scotland, Wales, Northern Ireland and Eire. A Link House Publication, available from newsagents.

WATERWAY USERS COMPANION (The British Waterways Board). Another invaluable publication, this one covers all the waterways for which the Board are responsible. It lists British Waterways Board area and section offices, and hire-boat and hotel boat firms on the waterways, where pumping out and sanitary stations are situated, recreation facilities on reservoirs, angling organisations on the Board's waterways, clubs and societies interested in the waterways and reservoirs, and other useful facts. It also has a clear description of how to get safely through locks. Available from the Board's offices at Melbury House, Melbury Terrace, London NW1 6JX.

Maps

It is possible to have a perfectly enjoyable boating holiday without a map but the possession of one can add considerably to one's enjoyment, for they can indicate the whereabouts of a great variety of sites and sights, museums, stately homes, pleasure grounds, nature reserves and even pubs.

Route planners, too, are invaluable. They can help the holidaymaker make the best use of his hire period by ensuring that he does not waste time getting lost or travelling over routes that do not interest him.

The hire-boat agencies and operators have a good selection of maps and route planners printed especially for them so that they pinpoint things likely to be of some interest to holidaymakers, as well as indicating the agencies' boatyards and other amenities. Blakes' *Holiday Map of the Norfolk Broads*, for instance, has a detailed map of the whole Broadland system, street plans round the waterway area for eleven towns and a distance chart. Hoseasons' *Cruising Map of Canals and Rivers of England and Wales* includes a route planner and time calculators as well as a map of the whole system and smaller maps showing some sections, including the Birmingham Canal Navigations, in closer detail. These are just two examples of the wide variety of maps the agencies can sell you. They usually list them in their brochures, or they can send you a list of what they have to offer.

Recommended maps to look out for include:

IMRAY'S MAP OF THE INLAND WATERWAYS. A large, fold-out map very good for coming to terms with the whole system. It includes the unnavigable waterways.

NAVIGATOR ROUTE PLANNER (Belmont Press). This shows the inland waterways system, with mileages, numbers of locks and estimated time needed to navigate each section.

NAVIGATOR STRIP MAPS (Belmont Press). A good series covering most of the major waterways, to a scale of two miles to one inch.

NICHOLSON GUIDES TO THE WATERWAYS (Robert
Nicholson Publications). There are five titles in this
useful series of softcover booklets: South East, North
West, South West, North East, and Midlands. The books
are based on half-inch-to-one-mile strip maps of the canal
systems and show essential navigation information –
tunnels, locks, bridges, junctions – as well as boatyards
and pubs. Places to eat and drink in the area are listed and
basic notes about the towns and villages en route are
included.

Stanford, the map publishers, include in their list a
*CANOEING MAP OF ENGLAND AND WALES,
CANOEIST'S MAP OF IRELAND, MAP OF THE INLAND
WATERWAYS, MAP OF THE NORFOLK BROADS*, and
MAP OF THE RIVER THAMES. These are fold-out maps
to very detailed scales (the Thames map is 1½ inches to
the mile and the Broads map 1¼ inches to the mile) and
are very useful.

Books

THE BOOK OF THE THAMES by Mr and Mrs S.C. Hall
(Charlotte James Publishers). A facsimile reprint of a
book first published in 1859. All the delightful wood
block engravings of the original have been retained. The
text, which follows the river from its source out to sea, is
full of splendid diversions into history, natural history,
anecdote and gossip.

BRITISH CANALS by Charles Hadfield (David and
Charles). The standard general history, now in its sixth
edition. It is available in both hardcover and paperback
editions.

BROADMANSHIP by Richard Simpkin (Barrie and

Jenkins). A wide-ranging introduction to cruising on the Broads.

CANAL AND RIVER CRUISING (Know the Game series, EP Publishing Ltd). A snip at under £1.00. In its forty pages this little book, which was produced in collaboration with the Inland Waterways Association, covers just about everything the first-time waterways holidaymaker is likely to want to know.

CANALS ARE GREAT by Peter L. Smith (Enterprise Publications). As this little booklet is aimed specifically at children it is a pity it is not more attractively designed; it looks a bit dull and text-bookish. On the other hand, it is well written and is full of interesting material. It also assumes that children are perfectly capable of manoeuvring boats through locks – and has photos to prove it. Includes projects which will get children really involved in their waterway holiday.

CANALS OF THE BRITISH ISLES (David and Charles). A complete range of regional histories, many of them written or edited by Charles Hadfield, whose pleasant style and enormously wide and deep knowledge of the subject makes his books a pleasure to read. There are ten titles currently in print in the series, but the whole series is readily available in public libraries.

CANOEING COMPLETE edited by Brian Skilling (Kaye and Ward). A classic on the subject. Recently revised, this book contains sections of all aspects of the sport, all written by experts, and includes a chapter on inland touring.

DISCOVERING LOST CANALS by Ronald Russell (Shire Publications). Mr Russell has also published a detailed history of the lost canals of England and Wales, but this little book is a more than adequate introduction to the subject. It describes in detail some sixteen derelict canals whose remains may still be traced by the enthusiast.

HOLIDAY CRUISING ON INLAND WATERWAYS by Charles Hadfield and Michael Streat (David and Charles). This is out of print but you should be able to find it in public libraries. A practical book, it includes sections on buying, hiring or converting your own boat.

HOLIDAY CRUISING ON THE BROADS AND FENS by L.A. Edwards (David and Charles). This book is also out of print which is a pity because it is an excellent read and full of invaluable practical information about cruising, notes on natural history and some social history. Most public libraries have it on their shelves, however, so look out for it.

INLAND WATERWAYS OF GREAT BRITAIN by L.A. Edwards (Imray, Laurie, Norie and Wilson). The standard reference book on the subject. First published in 1939, it has been substantially revised and updated several times since and now contains a wealth of statistics for every section of inland waterway in Great Britain. (It does not include Northern Ireland.)

INTRODUCING INLAND WATERWAYS (David and Charles). This softcover book by Charles Hadfield is still available in many canal-side shops and regular bookshops, although it has to some extent been superceded by Mr Hadfield's more recent INLAND WATERWAYS (also published by David and Charles). Both are excellent introductions to the story of inland waterways, and cover all aspects of the subject including the historical background, the present-day work of saving and restoring canals, and practical advice on boat handling, coping with locks, and joining societies.

NARROW BOAT by L.T.C. Rolt (Eyre Methuen). This is a real classic: an account of a trip by narrow boat in the early 1940s which alerted people to the possibility and desirability of restoring the old canal system. Available in hardcover and paperback versions.

THE SHELL BOOK OF INLAND WATERWAYS by Hugh McKnight (David and Charles). This book is practically an encyclopedia and contains chapters on most aspects of the subject, plus a detailed gazetteer.

THE STORY OF OUR CANALS by Carolyn Hutchings (Ladybird Books). This is a delightful book for young children and tells how and why canals came to be built, as well as describing the engineering feats involved. It is illustrated in full colour throughout and includes a waterways map and a guide to locking.

This is just a tiny sample of the wealth of books available on all aspects of waterway history, development and use.

The Inland Waterways Association, 114 Regent's Park Road, London NW1 8UQ has a well-stocked bookshop where you can browse happily; or the IWA can send you a complete stock list of titles and prices, including packing and postage.

The British Waterways Board, Melbury House, Melbury Terrace, London NW1 6JX also has a bookshop and information centre which stocks guides, books, posters and postcards.

The Baker Street Bookshop, 33 Baker Street, London W1 has a good range of boating books, particularly books about inland waterways.

Captain O.M. Watts, 49 Albemarle Street, London W1, has a fine selection of books covering all aspects of sailing. (They are also good for sailing clothes and equipment.)

Boating For The Disabled

Until 1980, anybody physically handicapped enough to

need a wheelchair would have experienced considerable difficulty in arranging a lengthy boating holiday for themselves and their family. Companies which specialise in arranging canal and river trips for disabled people and their companions usually do so for groups for a few hours or a day.

Early in 1980 the Spinal Injuries Association launched their first purpose-built narrow boat. Called *Kingfisher*, the sixty-foot craft was specially designed, adapted and built in consultation with the Association by Willow Wren Cruisers of Rugby. It has lifts at bow and stern, so that someone in a wheelchair can board at the bow, wheel themselves right through the boat and onto the stern lift which will raise them to the right height from which to steer the boat. The hydraulic assisted steering has a special release valve just in case something goes wrong. There is a galley sink at the right height for someone in a wheelchair and a specially designed lavatory. The boat is advertised as sleeping six, but in fact was adapted early in its first season to take another berth near the disabled person's berth, just in case he or she has to be turned in bed at night.

The only drawback to this holiday narrow boat for a disabled person and his family is that there is only one boat. The S.I.A. has had to limit its hire to Association members; even so, bookings have been heavy, and the waiting list is long.

Bookings for *Kingfisher* are handled by: Willow Wren Hire Cruisers Limited, Rugby Wharf, Consul Road, off Forum Drive, Rugby, Warwickshire CV21 1NR.

Other companies which arrange trips for the disabled are: B & M CHARTERS, Willsbrook, Raglan, Gwent (tel. 0291 690201). This company has a fifty-two-foot cruiser, on which they take parties of twenty to fifty on two-hour trips on the Monmouthshire and Brecon Canal.

British Waterways Board, Canal Office, Delamere Terrace, London W2 6ND (tel. 01 286 6101).

London's Regent's Canal is the cruising area for the Board's special boat trips for the disabled, in a broad-beam waterbus with plenty of room inside. The route takes in Little Venice, the Maida Hill tunnel, Regent's Park, and skirts the Zoo.

Heulwen-Sunshine, c/o Mrs Millington, 3 Church Road, Welshpool, Powys (tel. Welshpool 2563). This is another narrow boat specially designed for the disabled and their companions. The boat with its full-time crew operates on the seven-mile restored stretch of the Montgomery Canal, near Welshpool, and is paid for – hire fee, tea and biscuits etc. – by the Prince of Wales Committee. The boat was designed for day trips, so has no sleeping berths. It can take a party of up to eleven disabled people and their helpers, who may take the boat for a full day, from 9 am to 5 pm, bringing their own packed lunches.

The river at Henley-on-Thames, the popular Oxfordshire town and scene of the annual Henley Royal Regatta

CHAPTER 3

The Boat Hire Companies

As you will have gathered by now, this country is very well
served by companies hiring out holiday boats, and there
are not too many stretches of navigable inland waterways
with holiday traffic potential which have nothing on
offer.

In the previous chapter there is a list of the main
publications in which to find hire companies. Occasionally,
a company will go out of business, perhaps because it was
operated by one person who has sold out because of
illness, or will change the nature of its business – from
hiring to selling boats, perhaps – after these publications
have gone to press, but on the whole you should have no
difficulty in using them to track down five or six companies which seem to fulfil your requirements.

The booking agencies can offer you a wide range of
companies in all parts of the country, of course, but there
are still a large number of reputable companies operating
independently of them.

The Association of Pleasure Craft Operators, 35a High
Street, Newport, Salop, TF10 8JW, is a trade body with
some 150 boat operators on its list. The Association has
adopted the British Waterways Board's standards of
operation (indeed, the Association helped draft them)
which are observed by all their operators. They can
supply a complete list of their member companies on
request.

When looking for a narrow boat operator, don't forget
the British Waterways Board themselves. Apart from the
day trips they operate on the Regent's Canal in London,
the Board have two bases from which they hire out some
very attractive narrow boats, complete with all the facilities
and extras to be found among the best boat hire com-

panies. The Board's bases are at Nantwich on the Shropshire Canal in Cheshire and at Hillmorton on the Oxford Canal (North) 2½ miles south of Rugby. Address for brochures and bookings is: British Waterways Board, Hire Cruiser Booking Office, Nantwich Basin, Chester Road, Nantwich, Cheshire CW5 8LB.

Some Independent Operators

A selection of independent companies operating in the more specialised corners of the industry:

Camping Boats

Companies not operating through agencies, who have camping boats for hire, are:

Boat and Butty Company, 101 Kingsley Road, Frodsham, Cheshire WA6 6SJ. Tel: Frodsham (0928) 33522. The company takes private bookings for their craft, though most hirings are done through Educational Cruises.

Foxton Boat Services, Foxton Bottom Lock, near Market Harborough, Leicestershire. Tel: Kibworth 2285. This company has pairs of twelve-berth camping boats, plus twelve-berth butties, licensed for all British Waterways Board waterways, with licenses obtainable for other waterways (four-six weeks' notice needed), cancellation insurance plan offered.

Stroudwater Carriers Ltd., 7 Stringers Close, Radborough, Stroud, Gloucestershire. Tel: Stroud 2915. One camping boat, operating on the River Severn.

Threefellows Carrying, Sawley Lock House, Sawley, Long Eaton, Nottinghamshire. Tel: Sandiacre 399 747. Camping boats on the River Trent.

Warwickshire Flyboat Company, Shop Lock, Stockton, Warwickshire. Tel: Coventry 334228. One pair of camping boats, operated by a former school teacher. The pair are also available through Educational Cruises.

Canoes

Both canoes and kayaks may be hired by the day for canoeing on inland waterways. Many canoe clubs and outdoor activity centres will hire out their canoes, plus paddles, life-jackets, splash covers etc. if they are not required for courses or by club members.

The British Canoe Union, Flexel House, 45-47 High Street, Addlestone, Weybridge, Surrey. Tel: Weybridge (0932) 41341. Can supply a complete list of canoe clubs in Britain.

Canoe camping holidays, with a group of enthusiasts, are a splendid way of discovering Britain by canoe. Organisations which run them include:
The Canoe Camping Club, a sub-section of the Camping Club of Great Britain, 11 Lower Grosvenor Place, London SW1W 0EY. Tel: 01 828 1012.
The Holiday Fellowship, 142 Great North Way, Hendon, London NW4.
The *Youth Hostels Association* Adventure Holidays, Trevelyan House, St Albans, Herts. Tel: St Albans 55215.

Companies and organisations which hire out canoes include:
Dartmoor Expedition Centre, Rowden, Widecombe-in-the-Moor, Newton Abbott, Devon TQ13 7TX. Tel: Widecombe 249.
Eagle Canoe Club, Heigham Street, Norwich, Norfolk. Tel: Norwich 44051.
PGL Young Adventure Ltd., 32-34 Station Street, Ross-on-Wye, Hereford. Tel: Ross-on-Wye 4211.

Whitewater Sports, Guildford Road, Woking, Surrey. Tel: Woking 72426.

Horse-Drawn Boats

I hesitated over including these, as horse-drawn boat trips tend to be ad hoc affairs. Several companies withdrew their services in 1980 and could not confirm whether they would be starting up again in 1981. One company which is operating in 1981 is:

Kennet Horseboat Company, Greenham Island, Mill Lane, Newbury, Berkshire. Tel: Newbury 44154. The company runs day trips only on the Kennet and Avon Canal, with a broad-beam craft pulled by Primrose or Princess.

Hotel Boats

There are some sixteen boat companies operating hotel boats in England and Wales. Most are represented by Boat Enquiries Ltd or by the Central Booking Agency for Inland Waterways Holidays. One independent operator is:

Inland Cruising Company Ltd, The Boatyard, Braunston, near Daventry, Northants, NN11 7HT. Rugby 890325. The company operates one pair of hotel narrowboats, *Mallard* and *Dabchick*, carrying twelve passengers and a crew of four each.

Thames Sailing Barge

The booking agencies, Hoseasons and Blakes, each operate two sailing barges. An independent company is:

Anglian Yacht Services, 28 Spital Road, Maldon, Essex. Tel: Maldon 52290. A superb red-sailed Thames sailing barge, or spritsail barge, the *Reminder*, built in 1929 has been refitted and rerigged for charter sailing. She takes up to twelve passengers and a crew of three. Passengers are encouraged to take part.

The Booking Agencies

There are five main booking agencies in the holiday boat hire industry in this country. None charges its customers any agency or booking fee; they take a commission from the boat companies for whom they act as agent. The following notes are in alphabetical order, with no preferences intended. In fact, I found them all very friendly and helpful when I contacted them for this book.

BLAKES HOLIDAYS, Wroxham, Norwich, NR12 6DH. Tel: Wroxham (06053) 2141. Telex: 97114.
Blakes is the oldest of the booking agencies, having begun as a family business on the Broads in Edwardian times. Broadlands, where they have nearly forty companies operating at nineteen centres, is still their biggest area of operations. They have been on the English and Welsh canals since 1974, where their twenty-five operators have twenty-nine bases. Blakes are also a major presence on the Thames, Severn and Avon Rivers, on Loch Ness and the Caledonian Canal and the West Coast of Scotland, on the Grand Canal, River Barrow, Shannon and Lough Erne in Ireland, and in France, Greece and Holland. They have two Thames sailing barges, the *Marjorie* and the *Anglia*, operating from St Katherine's Dock, London.

Where Blakes differs from other agencies is in the fact that the company is owned by its operator-members. Their council is elected from among their members and it is this experienced group of people who vet applicants for membership. The quality and standards of performance of existing members are maintained by constant ad hoc visits from the company, and by prompt investigation of any complaints or problems notified by their customers.

Blakes Boating Holidays 1981 brochure is the 73rd annual edition. Printed in full-colour throughout and

54

giving detailed information including layouts of hundreds of boats, it is a different publication from Mr Harry Blake's 1908 version, which contained forty-three cabin yachts.

Blakes' customers are given a free holiday book covering the area of their chosen holiday. The Norfolk Broads Holiday Book, for instance, is a sixty-four page booklet containing a great deal of useful information which holidaymakers would be well advised to study before starting their holiday. There are small maps showing the location of bases, the rules of the river set out in easily assimilated form, notes on the safe handling of cruisers, dinghies, and yachts, where and how to moor, getting safely under Broads bridges. . . . a lot of good stuff, in fact. If you read through it before your holiday, you will be able to make a list of questions to be answered by the boatyard staff when you take over your boat.

Blakes also have for sale a selection of maps, route planners and other publications, including the Link House books and the Nicholsons Guides.

Examples of Blakes' 1981 prices are: a four berth motor cruiser from £120-£250 plus VAT and a six-berth cruiser from £140-£300 plus VAT. Highest prices operate in July and August.

BOAT ENQUIRIES Ltd, 43 Botley Road, Oxford, OX2 6ED. Tel: Oxford (0865) 511161. Telex: 83507.
This company has been in business for nearly twenty years and operates on the English and Welsh canal system, the Severn and Avon area, the Thames, and the Norfolk Broads. The self-drive cruisers and narrow boats operated by its independent boat companies offer much the same facilities and services as the other agencies and companies, and its hire fees and terms are also similar.

Where Boat Enquiries is different is in the fact that it can offer holidays in the specialised hotel boat market. While self-drive boats find the majority of their customers from families and groups of friends, the hotel boat holiday is an attractive proposition for single people or couples. Boat Enquiries' hotel boats include a broad-beam cruiser on the Broads, a hotel barge based in the East Midlands, and several pairs of hotel narrowboats.

Boat Enquiries publishes a colourful brochure every year, and its annual publication *A Lazy Man's Guide to Holidays Afloat* includes some interesting general articles about waterways holidays, all illustrated in colour and black and white, as well as the company's brochure bound in at the back.

1981 fees range from £135 to £155 per person for seven nights on a hotel boat. Self-drive hire fees are: £98–£207 including fuel for a two-berth cruiser; £106–£273 including fuel for a four-berth; £144-£380 including fuel for a six-berth; and £164–£425 for an eight-berth. These prices are for one week, and the highest price is for the height of the season.

CENTRAL BOOKING AGENCY FOR INLAND WATER-WAYS ACTIVITIES, 50 Main Street, Thornton, Leicester LE6 1AG. Tel: Bagworth (053 021) 230. Jerry and Angela Goodman have been operating this agency for three years now and, because it is not vast, are able to give their customers a service with an emphasis on personal help and advice. They can suggest routes that are not too difficult for first-time holiday boat hirers, gently discourage people away from trips which would require cruising for ten hours a day to get round, and will warn in advance of closures which might affect a route.

The Goodmans visit all the yards in their brochure at least once a year and try to pop in three or four times during the season as well. They don't have the same sort of link agreement with their yards as Blakes or Hoseasons, as the yards in their brochures are too spaced out, but they do ensure that all their yards have an adequate call-out service to deal with any breakdowns which may happen.

The Central Booking Agency brochure includes self-drive cruisers and narrow boats, hotel boats, and camping craft. The self-drive boat companies operate on the

A holiday boat base at Great Haywood, on the Staffordshire and Worcestershire Canal

Thames, the Severn and Avon, in the Fens, on the Broads, and on the Midlands and Shropshire canal networks. The attractive pairs of hotel boats they offer come from Canal Transport Services and the long-established Willow Wren company who also operate the camping boats in the Central Booking Agency brochure.

CBA also offer their customers a good selection of maps and route planners.

EDUCATIONAL CRUISES, 15 Main Street, Snarestone, Burton-on-Trent, Staffordshire DE12 7DB. Tel: Measham (0530) 71827. This company specialises in arranging holidays and educational cruises for parties in multiples of twelve up to sixty in number in narrowboat cruisers or campers, with butties. Parties have the choice of either self-drive boats or of a boat with an experienced skipper and crew, mostly the latter. Crew include people with teaching experience.

The campers have the old working boat hold covered with a strong canvas top, usually with perspex windows. Berths are double bunks in dormitory layout, with washing and cooking facilities: basic, but fine for kids.

The cruisers are more pricey, but the accommodation is more luxurious, often including shower, hot and cold running water, fridges etc. On both kinds of narrow boat, parties bring their own sleeping bags, but crockery, cutlery etc. is supplied.

Educational Cruises emphasise the 'togetherness' of this kind of holiday, with the young people learning to get on together as they undertake the cooking, washing up, tidying up of the boat and so on. The educational aspect comes not just in learning how to handle the boat, but also in studying the natural environment – animals, plants, birds and insects – of the countryside, the design and architecture of the canal systems and the science and mathematics of the engineering involved.

Like the other agencies and companies, Educational Cruises operates a Cancellation Insurance scheme and a personal accident and baggage insurance scheme.

Educational Cruises' hire fees for 1981 range from £165 to £245 per week for a twelve-berth camper with a boatman; and from £255–£356 per week for a twelve-berth cruiser (hotel boat) with a boatman.

HOSEASONS HOLIDAYS LTD, Sunway House, 89 Bridge Street, Oulton Broad, Lowestoft, Suffolk NR32 3LT. Tel: 0502 64991 (but see their brochure for Dial-a-Booking telephone numbers). Telex: 975189. The Hoseason family had their boat hire business on the Broads in the 1930s, and their holiday boat agency dates from 1945. The company now has more than 2700 boats in their current brochure. They have sixty Broads boat companies in their brochure, operating from seventeen Hoseason centres; six start points on the Fens; nineteen bases on the Thames; sixty-five boatyard start points on the English and Welsh canals; a relatively new base on Loch Lomond in Scotland and half a dozen starting bases on the Western coast of Scotland, plus bases on the Caledonian Canal and Loch Ness. In Ireland, there are Hoseason bases on the Shannon and the Erne waterways. Hoseason can also offer sailing holidays in the Mediterranean and on the inland waterways of France. Back in England, they offer holidays on two magnificent Thames sailing barges, the *Xylonite* and the *Ironsides*.

Hoseasons' main concern in Britain these days is not so much to increase the size of their operations – though they are doing this, too – as to 'improve the product' as the media men put it. They replace old boats with new on a regular basis, put household-size cookers in their boats wherever possible and add such luxuries as duvets on the berths and pressure cookers in the galley cupboard.

They are also making what they consider a natural progression of the family boating business into the more adventurous world of sea cruising.

All Hoseason customers get a free Holiday Hints Handbook for their area when they book and a Boat Manual, containing more detailed notes on boat handling and the individual characteristics of their boat, is given them when they arrive at the boatyard. They also have for sale a good range of maps and route planners.

Examples of Hoseasons' 1981 prices are: a four-berth motor cruiser from £110-£260 plus VAT and a six to seven-berth cruiser from £180-£390 plus VAT. The highest prices operate in July and August.

Making The Booking

First point: if you are under eighteen you cannot make a booking at all. If you are aged between eighteen and twenty-one, you may not be accepted as a customer. Check the brochure notes.

First Steps

You can make a reservation with all the agencies and with most independent hire companies by telephone, but your reservation will not be confirmed until you have sent in a completed booking form (printed in the back of all the brochures) and the total initial payment.

Your initial payment is the deposit on the boat, plus the Cancellation Plan cost. The Cancellation Plan cost is not optional with Blakes or Hoseasons, and is not returnable, but without it you could find yourself liable for the total hire charge in the event of cancellation. If you encounter a boat hire company that does not offer a cancellation plan or you cannot get insurance to cover you against cancellation, then be very wary.

Blakes and Hoseasons each print a table of the initial payments in their brochures (the payment varies according to the size and type of boat being hired); with Boat Enquiries the deposit is one-third of the total hire cost of the boat of your first choice; and with the Central Booking Agency it is one-third of the total hire cost of your first choice boat, plus VAT.

If you have not received confirmation of your booking within two weeks of sending in the completed form and your initial payment, you should get in touch with the agency/hire company at once. They are usually prompt in sending confirmation, and a two-week delay would suggest that your form has been lost in the post.

Final Payments

You will find that you are required to pay the balance of the hire fee plus the cost of extra charges and optional extras four to six weeks before the starting date of your holiday (up to eight weeks for holidays in Ireland). The balance is payable direct to the boatyard, *not* to the agency. In many cases, if you intend paying in cash rather than by cheque or credit card, you can hand over the money when you arrive to take over your boat.

Your final payment could be quite a hefty bill. The booking confirmation form will show you in detail what you have to pay. It can include:

Balance of the boat hire fee: about two-thirds of the total.

Fees for extra people.

Fees for pets (could be £4 or £5).

Fuel: the cost may be included in the hire fee. If not, reckon on about £25 for a week's cruising. You may get a refund if you set off with a full tank and it is not all used.

Bed linen (if not included in hire fee).

Television (if not included in hire fee).

Buoyancy aids (if not included in hire fee).

Rowing or sailing dinghy (on the Broads).

VAT on the total hire fee at current standard rate.

Security deposit (about £30): although boats are insured by their owners, the hirer is responsible for the first part of any damage caused. If the boat is returned in good condition, the security deposit is refunded. Please note, though, that the payment of a security deposit does not give you the freedom to cause any sort of damage you like on the waterways. You, as boat skipper, are responsible for any damage you may cause to waterway property, and you could well have to pay the bills if the British Waterways Board, for instance, submits them.

Outboard motor (for yachts).

Bicycle(s).

Extra licenses.

Sailing tuition (on the Broads): about £5 or £6 an hour.

Maps and guides.

Car parking: often free if you are willing to leave your car out in the open; there will probably be a charge of £3 or £4 for under-cover parking.

In addition to all these payments to be made to the boatyard, don't forget that you will also have to pay for any groceries delivered to your boat.

This could add up to a large bill, a fact which both Blakes and Hoseasons have recognised in their provision of 'time-payment schemes'. With Blakes, you can spread payment over a period to suit yourself, though the final payment must be made four weeks before the holiday starts. Hoseasons have a Budget Loan Plan under which you save a fixed sum each month on which interest is paid. You can withraw money against your deposit at any time, though there is a credit limit, of course, and you have to pay interest on the loan.

A Look At The Hire Conditions

If you are the sort of person who never looks at the small print in contracts you sign, do read the following. It is a summary of the agencies' booking conditions, and should alert you to problems which could arise:

Hire terms: these are per week. If the full balance of fees is not paid by the specified date, the boat company can re-let the boat for the hire period in question. It does not have to return the hirer's deposit.

Cancellation: If you cancel your booking, you are liable to pay the full amount due, however good the reason for cancellation seems to you. However, if the boat company is able to re-let your boat, you may only forfeit your booking deposit. This is where the Cancellation Plan cover offered by the agencies and most boat companies, comes in because they may insure you against having to pay. Under the Cancellation Plan, if you have already paid your fee in full when you have to cancel then this will be returned in full; if you have just made your initial payment, then the deposit fee will be returned to you. The major condition for the Cancellation Plan to operate is that your reason for cancelling must be valid. A simple change of mind by you or any member of your party is not acceptable and you, as the person signing the booking form, will be liable for the full amount.

You should always inform the agency/company at once if you have to cancel. As a matter of interest, under the Cancellation Plan acceptable reasons for cancelling your holidays are: death, injury, illness, maternity, jury service or redundancy (from work) of any member of your party, or as a result of death, injury or illness of a close relative or business associate, and this is confirmed by the appropriate certificate, provided they have all arisen since the initial booking was made.

Taking over the boat: the operator will give each hirer a trial run to explain the boat's controls and equipment and to check that the engine is in good order. After this, the hirer is responsible for any damage to the boat or loss of its equipment. The boat company will accept no responsibility for loss of time or for expenses occasioned by a break-down of the boat while it is in the hirer's possession. If you let the boat company know as soon as you can that something has gone wrong, then they will, of course, do everything they can to fix it as quickly as possible. Incidentally, the boat company is not liable to give their boat into your care. If they have good reason for not liking the look of you (you and your party may arrive roaring drunk) or they feel that you are not capable of handling the boat (perhaps you broke a leg and an arm falling off a horse or your motorbike last week), they can refuse to let you have the boat. They should, however, make full refund of any monies you have already paid over, and they would never refuse on frivolous or personal grounds, but only if they seriously believe that to let you have the boat could lead to a serious accident.

Accommodation: boats may not be occupied by more people than the number agreed on the booking form. Infringement of this rule, which is made for your safety, could mean an immediate termination of the hire and forfeit of fees paid.

Accidents: as the hirer of the boat, you are considered to be in charge of it and responsible for its safe and sensible navigation. No child may control the boat without the supervision of an experienced adult. If you do have an accident, or damage your boat, another boat or waterway property, you must obtain the name of the other boat involved and the names of its hirers and/or owner, and you should tell your operator as soon as possible. As in car accidents, don't admit liability – it could affect the insurance. The insurance could also be affected if the accident is considered to have happened because you did not make the proper signals or correct horn sounds, so make sure you know what they are. (See Chapter 5: In Charge.) If you damage waterway property, or cause an undue loss of water, you are responsible for any charges which the Waterway authorities may make and neither the security deposit you have paid nor the boat's own insurance frees you from this liability.

Damage to you, the boat, and its equipment: The operator is not responsible for death, personal injury, or loss or damage to your property unless these can be proved to have resulted from negligence on their part. Although the boat is insured, you as the hirer are responsible for it and its gear and equipment. You should report and may have to pay for any damage, or for lost or damaged equipment. The security deposit you pay before taking over the boat covers you for the first part of any insurance claim which the boat's owner might have to pay.

Restrictions on your use of the boat: Under no circumstances may you: tow other cruisers, cruise after dark, permit your boat to be taken out to sea (unless on the West Coast of Scotland you have made arrangements to do so).

I have already mentioned the matter of domestic electric appliances on hire boats, but please note that a ban on them is one of the conditions of hire.

Insurance

A hire-boat is a very valuable object, and a waterway holiday, like any other, can have dangers lurking, so it is well to be properly insured. You may find that your own family personal insurance policy also protects you while on holiday, or would do if you paid a small extra premium, so check with your insurance company in good time.

If you have no such insurance and want to be insured just for the duration of your holiday, then you can take out a policy through the agencies. The Cancellation Plan Insurance can be extended to a full-blown insurance cover for you and your party, covering you against the costs of cancelling a holiday, loss of baggage, loss of cash and personal accident while on holiday. Insurance forms are printed in the brochures.

Each member of the party who is to be covered by the insurance policy has to be named at the time you take it out, so if there are any changes in the composition of your party a week or two before the holiday, you should inform the insurance company.

The boat's owner will have insured her fully, but don't forget that you, as the hirer, have to pay the first part of any claim against the boat's insurance. In fact, you pay this in advance in the form of the security deposit you give the operators before you take over the boat; it is refunded to you if the boat returns to its yard in good order.

Licences

Hire-boats on the canal system are already licenced by their owners for cruising on British Waterways Board property, and cruisers on the Thames, the Broads and other rivers will have been registered wherever necessary. The holidaymaker taking on a hire-boat therefore has no need to worry about licences unless he intends cruising on waterways where the British Waterways Board licence is either not valid or reciprocal. Among canals where the British Waterways Board licence does not apply is the Rochdale Canal, an important link in the Cheshire Ring, and a special licence will have to be purchased. Operators and agencies can advise where extra licences are necessary and can also arrange to get them for you, though you must pay the additional fee. They need four to six weeks' warning, especially at the height of the season.

All private craft, from the smallest canoe to the largest cruiser, must be licenced or registered. The licence fee scale is complicated, and depends on the size of the craft, its means of propulsion, how long the licence is wanted for, whether the craft will be using locks or not, and other factors. Private boat owners requiring licence fees or wanting to get their craft registered should apply in time to the relevant authorities: the British Waterways Board for canals and some inland rivers; the Port and Haven Commissioners for the Broads, the Thames Water Authority, Thames Conservancy division, for the Thames, and various local authorities for other rivers and waterways.

Water Crowfoot.

CHAPTER 4

Buying Your Own Boat

Buying a boat is much like buying your own house. There is considerable capital outlay at the beginning, followed by smaller payments for insurance, licences and registration fees, repairs and maintenance, running costs, mooring fees and so on, for ever afterwards.

On the other hand, the boat is your own. You can take her somewhere different each holiday, free of hotel bills, and you can adapt her to suit exactly the requirements of you and your family. It has become increasingly common, too, for two or three people to share the cost of buying and maintaining a boat. This will work perfectly well provided that the terms of the arrangement are set out clearly and precisely in advance: who pays for what and, perhaps most important, who uses the boat when. Group ownership will not work if every member of the group wants to use the boat for the school holidays in August.

You must be clear in your own mind at the outset why you want to buy a boat. If you have had no experience of cruising or sailing, but just like the idea and can imagine yourself at the wheel, yachting cap at a jaunty angle, gin and tonic in hand, then you really should delay your purchase until you have had some practical experience. Buying the wrong boat can be a very costly mistake.

Having read this far, you will know that gaining experience can be easy enough: cruisers, narrow boats, sailing cruisers and yachts can all be hired, and tuition is readily available. You may also have boat-owning friends who will be happy to take you out a few times, pointing out the traps for the unwary, and giving you a few practical lessons.

This kind of experience will also help give you an idea of the kind of boat you want, though this point will be dictated to a degree by where you intend doing most of your boating. If you live in the middle of England miles from the sea, but close to the vast canal network, and you hope to use the boat most weekends rather than just two or three times in the summer, then your best buy might be a small cruiser or a narrow boat kept on moorings not too far from home. If you are going to be a solo sailor or have just one companion along, then a small boat which could be trailed anywhere, even to Europe, could be the one for you.

Once the type of boat is decided on, the next question to be answered is: What dimensions? Length, draught, beam and headroom must all be taken into account, bearing in mind the number of people likely to be aboard on most trips. Dimensions become vital considerations if the boat is to be used on the English and Welsh canals, as it will have to go through narrow and/or short locks, under low bridges, through narrow tunnels and round tight bends.

The question of the engine – inboard or outboard, petrol or diesel, low or high horsepower – is also of importance. As most people's first boat is at the smaller end of the scale, under 25 feet, an outboard engine is likely to be given preference. Boats with outboard engines cost less to build than those with inboards, which may be another deciding factor. The type of water on which the boat is to sail is important, too. A boat to be used on the canals, which lack tide or currents, will not require as powerful an engine as a boat operating in strong tidal waters where reserves of power are essential.

Finding exactly the right boat is a business which may give the first-time buyer a sleepless night or two. It is always a good thing to visit several boatyards, read magazines to discover the range available, the prices being asked, and visit exhibitions like the Earls Court Boat Show where you can see many kinds of boat gathered under one roof and can talk to their makers. It is all part of 'getting your eye in' and will also alert you to the sort of questions you should be asking the seller when you have narrowed your search down to one or two boats.

If it is your first boat, you would be well advised to buy it, whether new or second-hand, from a reputable boatyard or marine chandler. You will then have the advice and expertise of professional people to call on, and a good back-up service if you need it.

As in buying a house, so in buying a boat you will need the services of a surveyor. This could be a qualified marine surveyor or perhaps a friend with plenty of boating experience. The former will charge a fee for his services but will give you a professional judgement on the condition of the boat you are considering.

Boatyards may have boats at various stages of completion on offer, from factory-built craft complete in all basics including cooker, fridge, toilet, upholstered berth and seating cushions, down to the basic hull and cabin top, which you have to fit out yourself. A relatively new method of pre-fabricating the entire cabin unit of a narrow boat, including the floor, sides, top and bulkheads, which is then lowered in one unit on to the steel hull, has appreciably reduced the cost of some of these craft.

You could, of course, have a boat built to your own specifications, though this is something better left until you have had experience of handling several boats and know exactly what you want. It is a pretty expensive business, too. The custom-built narrow boat *Kingfisher*, owned by the Spinal Injuries Association, which I mentioned in Chapter 2, cost £25,000 to build and fit out.

Second-hand craft can be bought at boatyards. The yards may have taken them in part-exchange on a new boat, or they may have been put into the boatyard's hands for selling, as houses are sold through estate agents. These latter are called 'brokerage' sales, and you should be a little more wary of these than second-hand boats which the boatyard is selling on its own account. Most of them will be perfectly all right but, as with houses and used cars, it is a case of 'buyer beware'.

Second-hand boats may also be bought from hire-fleets at the end of the season. Some hire-fleets replace their craft at regular intervals and, usually around July, advertise the boats they will be wanting to sell in September or October. Although these boats will have been well-used they will also have been well-maintained, and will have been built and fitted out to stringent standards of design and safety.

Even if your boat comes from the factory complete with all the basics like engine, berths, toilet, cooker and refrigerator, you will still have a long list of extras to buy before she is completely fitted out. These could cost several hundred pounds and are a major factor to be considered when deciding if you can afford to buy a boat.

The external extras can include ropes (a minimum of three, each 30 to 50 feet long), mooring irons, an anchor, navigation lights, a horn, boat hooks, fire extinguishers (needed below in the galley, too), life jackets or buoyancy aids, perhaps a floating cushion or two, a life-belt and fenders. You may also need a dinghy if your boat is based on the Broads or has a harbour mooring.

In the cabin, you will probably want to provide the boat with its own crockery, cutlery, pots and pans, kitchen utensils and bedding (usually sleeping bags), rather than pack this sort of gear up at home every time you use the boat.

Unless your boat is small enough to be kept on a trailer in the front garden, you will need permanent moorings for it. These can be expensive, especially in boatyards and marinas with many facilities, including water supplies, fuel and chandlery, as well as jetties and pontoons to be maintained. Mooring fees are usually calculated by the foot per week. Navigation authorities and organisations like the British Waterways Board can provide lists of moorings in their areas, including off-the-line private sites.

CHAPTER 5

In Charge

Taking Over

Your family or party of friends may look a pretty un-nautical bunch when you have unloaded them and their holiday gear on to the boatyard mooring stage; but don't worry, a bit of careful planning and by the end of a week, you will all feel you could cope with the *QE2* – or just about.

Of course, you have arrived at the boatyard free of worries about home, haven't you? You have stopped the milk and newspaper, made arrangements for the cat, switched off everything in the house that should be switched off, locked the back door . . . and left the name of your boat and the address and telephone number of the boatyard with a neighbour or relative, just in case of emergencies?

You may already have sorted out amongst yourselves what everyone's station in life is going to be for the next week or two. To quote Hoseasons *Holiday Hints Handbook*: 'The Captain is in charge of everything. The Mate is second in command and shares responsibility with the Captain. In a small crew the Mate might also be the Ship's Cook (this sounds as if mother is going to be given two full-time jobs to do – as usual). The Purser is in charge of money and shopping; the Chief Engineer is in charge of the engine and refilling with fuel and water; the Steward is in charge of the cabins; the Leading Seaman is in charge of keeping the upper deck clean and tidy, anchoring, and the forward moorings; the Able Seaman is in charge of fenders; and the Ship's Boy helps where he is most needed.'

A lift bridge on the Prees arm of the Llangollen Canal

Right then. You have been shown your boat and you are all aboard. Having looked her over to get your bearings, the first thing to do is to unpack and stow away your gear. This will enable you to put empty suitcases and bags in the boot of your car, or, if you can, leave them at the boatyard. They will take up precious room if you keep them on board. Never take anything on a boating holiday that you won't need as space is always at a premium.

On a self-drive hire-boat holiday the inventory is so detailed that each person need only bring personal clothing, towels, toilet kit and one or two personal 'things to do' (camera, books, binoculars, drawing block and pencils, fishing tackle). Everyone's personal clothing should include a pair of non-slip or rope-soled shoes (tennis and other rubber-soled shoes won't do, as they slip on a wet deck), a couple of warm sweaters and a waterproof outer covering (anorak, cagoule, oilskin, mackintosh). Apart from these, informal clothing is the rule, with perhaps something smart in case you have an evening out ashore.

Items to bring for the party as a whole should include at least one good torch (for coming back to the boat at night along the towpath), matches, corkscrew, bottle-opener, stout pen knife, sewing kit, first aid kit, tea towels, maps and route planners, a couple of packs of cards and pens and pencils. Don't forget to put toilet paper on your shopping list.

Having got your gear stowed away, the next thing to do is to check over the inventory to make sure everything the operator says is on your boat can be found. If you find yourself at the end of the holiday having your security deposit docked for missing cutlery or the boathook, it is no good saying then that you did not have them when you started out.

This job out of the way, you will then be ready to take in everything the boatyard staff have to tell you about your boat and how to handle her. Make sure that at least one member of the party is fully aware of how the engine and other mechanical equipment works, how to switch on and off the main gas supply and how to switch over from an empty to a full gas cylinder.

Check where the fuel and water come aboard and how to gauge the quantity you have.

Check that you know where the deck pump-out fitting for the toilet is situated.

Make sure that there is a correctly-fitting buoyancy aid or life jacket aboard for every member of the party. Non-swimmers, especially children, should wear these all the time they are on deck.

If you are cruising on canals you will need a windlass, or lock key, to get through locks (the windlass raises the lock gate paddles). Make sure you have it, and never leave it behind anywhere. It is probably the most vital piece of deck equipment on the boat.

Living In A Confined Space On Water

No matter how large your boat, you are not going to have as much room as you are accustomed to at home, which is why it is essential to be extra tidy and shipshape: a place for everything and everything in its place is the rule both in the cabin and saloon and on deck.

On deck, mooring ropes should always be neatly coiled. A heap of rope is dangerous, someone could trip over it, and inefficient because it may have to be disen-tangled and unknotted in a hurry when you need it for tying up, (you may have to throw it up to a lock-keeper for instance). Noticeable things about privately or pro-fessionally owned boats include the fact that they are usually spotlessly clean with paint and brasswork shining, and that ropes are always neatly, and even decoratively, coiled. A narrow boat fashion is to have the mooring ropes laid over the cabin top with the coils hanging neatly down the side.

The boat hook, shaft and mop should be laid neatly along the top, out of the way but within easy reach.

Everyone will be happy in a confined space provided they know what they should be doing and where they should be during such specific operations as mooring, going through a lock or negotiating things like bridges and tunnels. Two important rules: never allow anyone to sit on the top of the boat when going under bridges, and never allow anyone to dangle their legs over the side when locking or mooring.

As for the dog: narrow boat dogs seem to be a special breed, sure-footed and active. Your own pet may not be, and unless he is kept under control, he could become just one more thing for you to have to keep an eye on. He is probably safe enough on a narrow boat, though it is a good idea to keep him on a lead attached to something solid when you are mooring or locking. Sailing boats are a different matter. I know a charming little beagle who slid off the foredeck of his owner's yacht when it heeled over in the Solent, and he found there was nothing for his claws to get a grip on. Fortunately his lead was a strong one and properly attached to the boat so he was hauled aboard none the worse for his adventure, apart from too much seawater.

Caring For Your Boat

The boat you have taken over is a very valuable object: it could well be worth more on the open market than your house.

If you are careful to follow the rules of the river, to keep clear of other craft and to moor and lock correctly, the chances are that you won't so much as scratch the paintwork on the hull, while wearing soft-soled shoes on board will protect the deck.

This leaves the engine and other mechanics of the boat. Every boat operator will give you a list of daily checks which should be carried out faithfully to ensure that the engine runs well for the whole trip. Ignoring these simple checks could lead to breakdowns, which are always a time-consuming nuisance and can be dangerous.

If you read carefully through the following list of daily checks which Blakes recommend in their Holiday Books, then you will know what you must go over with the boat operator when you take over:

Every morning, before starting off, check:

1. The engine oil level. This is usually done with a dipstick, and should show 'full'.
2. The water level in the header tank, if one is fitted.
3. The stern gland. Where this is fitted, screw down the grease cap one turn. If it is fully down, refill with grease.
4. The weed strainer on the cooling water intake, if your boat has a water-cooled engine. This could well have got fouled up, preventing water pumping readily through the cooling system. Many canal cruisers and narrow boats have air-cooled engines, so the problem does not arise.
5. The fuel level. This is checked on most boats with a dipstick, though a few have gauges.
6. The fresh water tank; running out can cause an air lock in the system.
7. Bilge: pump out if necessary, unless there is oil.

Once you are under way, check:

1. Oil pressure.
2. The circulation of the cooling water.

The weed hatch is another item for you to know all about, as you get at the propellers through it. If you do have to take off the weed hatch cover to remove anything –plastic bags are a great hazard – which may have fouled up the propellers, remember to replace it and its rubber seal once you have sorted out the problem. Boats have been known to sink because their weed hatch was left uncovered. If your boat does not have a weed hatch, then you may have to get help. Some people manage to clear the propeller with a boat hook or even a bread knife, but it may not be so simple. Never try to clear the propeller before you have switched off the engine and removed the key.

The starter motor, as I have said, usually has a simple

button or key operation. If you do find that the engine does not start readily, you should have the starter checked over, as too much use can flatten the battery.

Cruising and sailing are not unlike driving a car. At first there seem to be so many things to remember and to try to synchronise that the hapless person 'in charge' of the boat may think that he will never get it all together. After a bit of practice and some experience, actions and reactions will start to become automatic and everything will be much more relaxed.

If the first time holidaymaker can familiarise himself with basics like the rules of the river, hints on mooring and locking, safety rules and so on before he even steps aboard his boat, he will be well on the way to a trouble-free holiday.

Rules Of The Rivers And Canals

The busier the waterway, the more important it is to know thoroughly the rules which govern all craft using it. In the event of an accident, ignorance of the basic rules is no excuse. Here is a summary of the rules that everyone in charge of a boat must know and observe.

Keep to the right: on a narrow river or canal, this usually means keeping to the right of centre rather than sticking to the right-hand bank or you may go aground. It certainly means that if you are passing a boat coming in the opposite direction you move over to the right so that the boats pass portside (left side) to portside.

Giving way: motor cruisers and sailing cruisers with engines running should give way to sailing yachts. Sailing yachts, on the other hand, should remember that in narrow channels some cruisers with deep draughts may not be able to pull right over. They should also remember that larger motor vessels like car and passenger ferries cannot manoeuvre as quickly as can a small yacht nor may their master be able to see from the bridge that a small

This photograph clearly shows the towpath and the unprotected edge which are memorable features of the Pontcysyllte aqueduct on the Llangollen Canal

yacht is sailing under his bow. The British Waterways Board bye-law covering this point says 'every vessel approaching any ferry shall reduce speed, and if necessary stop, and thereafter navigate so as not to obstruct or interfere with the effectual working of the ferry'.

Sailing boats running free should give way to ones sailing close-hauled or tacking against the wind.

All pleasure craft should give way to working craft or those towing other craft.

Passing and overtaking: yacht skippers may 'wave on' cruisers when they wish to be overtaken or passed. Cruiser skippers in doubt about this point should always slow down or even stop. Any vessel overtaking another should keep well clear of it.

Speed limits must be observed: maximum speed limit on canals is four miles per hour and on rivers eight miles per hour. On some canals, for example the Aire and Calder Navigation (except the Selby Canal), the New Junction Canal, the Sheffield and South Yorkshire Navigation, the Grand Union Canal from its junction with the Trent at Soar Mouth to West Bridge, Leicester, the Weaver Navigation and the Witham Navigation, the speed limit is six miles per hour.

Speed limits are imposed for reasons of safety and to protect river banks and river-side property. Excessive speed can cause waves heavy enough to wash away river banks, crash moored boats against jetties, or even tip over small craft like kayaks. If there is a breaking wave behind your boat you are moving much too fast.

You should always slow down when approaching fishermen on the banks, moored boats and small craft, and when you are passing under bridges. You only need once to have your own lunch or tea slopped all over the place when a speeding boat passes you on a mooring to get the message about this point.

Always watch out for notices which may impose special speed restrictions, and observe them implicitly.

Anyone failing to observe speed limits on waterways

could be liable to prosecution, and the British Waterways Board, the Port and Haven Commissioners on the Broads and the Thames Conservancy all have superintendents and officers appointed to enforce bye-laws and regulations.

Sound signals: all boats have a horn or whistle (not a bell). The horn or whistle is a navigation aid, enabling you to tell other craft what you are about to do. It is not there for children merrily to toot on as a pleasant diversion.

There are specific sounds meaning particular things, which you must be able to recognise:

One short blast: 'I am altering my course to starboard (that is, to the right).'

Two short blasts: 'I am altering my course to port' (that is, to the left).

Three short blasts: 'My engine is going astern.'

Four short blasts: 'I am unable to manoeuvre.'

One long blast: this is generally used as a *warning* signal, and would be applicable if you were moving along in conditions of poor visibility, such as fog, mist or heavy rain. The British Waterways Board bye-laws specify that such prolonged blasts should be made at intervals of not more than two minutes.

Some General Safety Advice

Many basic points about safety on boats have come up in the course of talking about other things: wearing the correct shoes, wearing life-jackets or buoyancy aids, keeping ropes neatly coiled, keeping off cabin tops when going under bridges, being careful in the way Calor gas is used, for instance. Others which should always be observed are:

Hold on when moving about the deck, particularly when the boat is moving. Grab-rails and other hand-holds are always near to hand, so use them.

Never try to leap across a gap when going ashore or getting aboard. It is all too easy to slip down between the boat and the mooring place.

Never use hands or legs to fend the boat off jetties, lock-sides, tunnels, bridges or other craft. They could get crushed. Use the boat hook. Incidentally, it is a good plan to detail a member of the crew to be in charge of fenders and ensuring that they are always in place.

Make sure that the lifebuoy, with which every hire boat is supplied, is to hand and not buried under towels, clothing or other equipment. You may need it quickly if someone falls into the water; throw the lifebuoy ahead of the person in the water, never at him.

You may have to use artificial respiration, the 'kiss of life', on someone who has fallen in, so make sure you are familiar with it. All hire-boats should have an artificial respiration chart prominently displayed on board, or you could get your own copy of the useful RoSPA booklet *On the Water, In the Water* before you go on holiday, (30p, 45p to non-members, plus 12p postage) from the Royal Society for the Prevention of Accidents, Cannon House, Priory Queensway, Birmingham B4 6BS. Tel: 021 233 2461.

Safely Through Locks

All locks on the Thames, and some on other rivers and the larger commercial canals, have lock-keepers. Their job is to supervise the lock, rather than to get you safely through it, though they themselves may sometimes feel more like policemen at busy crossings as they guide boats in and out on a summer Sunday. Where locks have lock-keepers, you should always follow their signals and directions.

Most locks the holidaymaker will encounter, especially on the canal system, are unattended and have to be operated by boat crews – that is, you and your family and friends. Locks are not at all difficult to operate, as you will find out once you have been through one or two, provided every crew member knows what his job is and how to do it. This is something which should be worked out in advance.

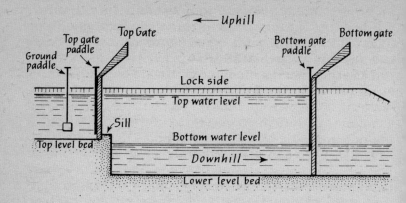

Uphill ←

Ground paddle | Top gate paddle | Top Gate | Bottom gate paddle | Bottom gate

Lock side

Top water level

Sill

Bottom water level

Top level bed

Downhill →

Lower level bed

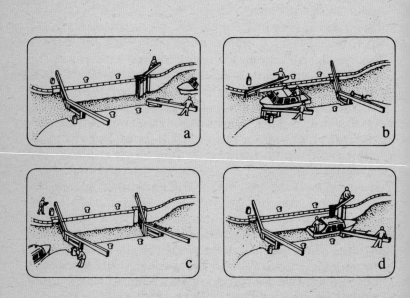

a

b

c

d

First of all, look at the section-drawing of a lock (opposite top), to see what the various parts are called.

When approaching a lock never hurry, there's plenty of time. On the other hand, never approach so slowly that you lose way altogether. If your propeller stops turning, you have no steerage and could find yourself drifting broadside on to the lock.

Now, a step-by-step drill for going through a lock:

Going up: (Diagram a)

1. Make sure the top gates and paddles are closed.
2. If the lock is full, empty it by raising the bottom paddles. You, or at least the crew member who has gone ahead, does this with the windlass or boat key, supplied by the boat operator.
3. Open the bottom gates and enter the lock. To open the gates, you *push* the balance beam over (experts say you get the best leverage by pushing with your rump) never *pull* it towards the lock edge, as the beam will push you into the lock. Once in the lock, move the boat up towards the top gates, but never right up against them as the bow could get caught on the gate. Loop the mooring ropes round bollards, stern rope first, to hold the boat steady. One crew member can usually manage both stern and bow ropes while standing on the lockside – you are not tying the boat up, merely holding her steady. In fact, you do not tie the boat up and abandon her; the ropes must be loose so that they can slacken off as the boat rises with the water level in the lock.

(Diagram b)

4. Close the bottom gates behind you and lower the paddles. This is also done with the windlass. Some books tell you to 'drop' the paddles, which means 'unwind gently', *not* 'drop with a crash'.
5. Open the top paddles to fill the lock.

6. Open the top gates and take your boat out.
7. Close the gates behind you and lower the paddles.

Going down: (Diagram c)

1. Make sure that the bottom gates and paddles are closed.
2. If the lock is empty, fill it by opening the top paddles.
3. Open the top gates and enter the lock, remembering to keep well clear of the lock gates.

(Diagram d)

4. Close the top gates behind you and lower the paddles.
5. Open the bottom paddles to empty the lock.
6. Open the bottom gates and take your boat out.
7. Close the gates behind you and lower the paddles.

Staircase Locks

These are one or more locks leading directly into another, with no pound between. There may be only a pair, or up to five, (the Bingley Five -Rise on the Leeds and Liverpool Canal is a famous one), or even eight, (on the Caledonian Canal in Scotland).

   Fortunately for the boat crew coming across them for the first time, staircase locks usually have a clear set of instructions displayed close by, or there is a lock-keeper to help.

   The main points to remember when tackling staircase locks are that you cannot enter a narrow lock staircase if there is already a boat coming towards you, and that you cannot empty a full lock into the lock below it if that one is also full. You could cause a bad flood. Lower locks must always be emptied first.

A boat descending the staircase at Foxton on the Grand Union Canal

Side Ponds

Some locks have side ponds beside them to help conserve water. With the side-pond system you empty the lock, half into the side pond and half into the lock below when coming down. When going up take half a lockful of water from a side pond and half from the lock above. On a complete locking, you will thus save about half a lockful of water.

General Rules

Always share a lock with other craft, if possible, as this helps preserve water supplies, always at a premium in canals.

If, when coming to a lock you find it is 'against' you and a boat is approaching from the other direction, wait and let it come through first. Each time you empty a lock you are sending nearly 25000 gallons of water away down the system. If enough people are careless with water in a really dry summer, they could be the cause of the canal having to be closed altogether.

Never leave a windlass on the paddle winding gear. If the gear's ratchet should slip or get knocked off, the windlass could fly off in a dangerously lethal way. Remember that some locks and their paddle gear have been in use for generations, and may be getting a bit delicate, so always use them gently, with care.

Always make sure that all gates and paddles are closed after you leave the lock.

Don't forget your windlass or mooring irons, which you may have had to use on the bank while waiting for the lock gates to open.

And, most important of all, if your boat does get caught in a lock, either on the top or bottom gates or because the mooring ropes have got themselves tight on a bollard, *close the paddles immediately* then think through the problem coolly and carefully. It is an excellent move to appoint one crew member to windlass duty: not only will he be solely responsible for the windlass's use and whereabouts, but he would remain on duty with it throughout the locking procedure, ready to stop the paddles at the first sign of trouble.

Bridges, Tunnels And Moorings

Getting Under Bridges And Through Tunnels

The main rule about *bridges* is that they should be approached with caution. They may be on a bend, so that a boat approaching from the other side cannot be seen. The boat nearest the bridge has right of way, though it is always better for a small boat to let a large boat through first, as the latter is less manoeuvrable.

Boat drill is:

1. Make sure that everyone and everything, including the dog, is off the deck or cabin top.
2. Lower the windscreen, canopy, and mast (if you have one).
3. Check that your boat has ample clearance. At low bridges on the Broads, for instance, the River Commissioners indicate the maximum height in feet between the underneath side of the bridge and water level.
4. Sound one blast of your horn as you approach the bridge.
5. If it is very windy, line up the boat a good distance away from the bridge so that you can judge in good time that you are steering a steady course.
6. Move steadily under the bridge; if you reduce speed too much you will lose steerage.

There are several types of moveable bridge on inland waterways, particularly the canals. Swing bridges, lifting bridges and bascule bridges (operated by a balance beam which one or two crew members have to pull down), may all be encountered. Many of them require a strong person to operate them, so do not leave this job to children: the bridge could easily swing back down on to the boat. You should always close these bridges once you have passed through.

If the bridge is a road bridge, rather than one enabling livestock to pass over the waterway, and does not have road barriers, then crew members should stand in the road to warn traffic that the bridge has been lifted or raised.

Tunnels encountered on canals need the same steady approach as bridges. Your boat must have a fixed head-light, a torch waved about in someone's hand will not do, and it should be directed towards the right-hand wall rather than down the centre of the tunnel, where it could blind a boat coming in the other direction.

If you are going through a tunnel wide enough for two boats (your maps and route planners will give the width of the tunnel as well as its length), ease over to starboard (the right) if you see another boat coming and *keep going*. If you slow down so much that you lose steerage you will very likely find yourself drifting into the path of the on-coming boat.

A narrow tunnel which will only take boats in one direction at a time may have a tunnel-keeper to tell you when to proceed, or there may be a timetable stating the times at which boats may go through in each direction. With a short tunnel, you will be able to see for yourself if a boat is coming the other way.

Tunnels can be rather wet places, with water dripping from the roof, so everyone should wear a waterproof coat or jacket, and items which could spoil if wet – cameras, radios, books and maps – should be put away in the cabin.

Canoeists are not permitted to use tunnels: being unpowered craft, canoes could get mown down. The best they can hope for is a lift aboard another boat.

Mooring

Like locking, mooring is not a difficult operation. It is

88

perhaps easier on canals than on the Broads, or other open stretches of water where there may be tides, currents and wind to allow for, but it is still a relatively simple operation.

Choosing a mooring place is certainly not a problem. On the canal system, and most rivers, you may moor almost anywhere on the towpath side, though not on the other side, much of which may be private. Of course, you may find many undesirable places, even on the towpath side: they may be too near railway lines, factories or other noisy buildings. And there are places where boats should not moor – close to locks, bridges, bends or weirs, for instance, or in a short pound (which is considered to be a pound where both locks are clearly visible). Never tie up to navigation posts, notices, or next to water or fuel points. Avoid fields full of cows: they are very inquisitive and you may wake at five in the morning to the sounds of them chomping on your mooring ropes. Avoid railway embankments and road over-passes, as they can be noisy.

If your first attempts at mooring can be made against quiet grassy banks, so much the better, as you are less likely to damage the boat. Slow down and approach your chosen mooring site carefully, making sure the water is not too shallow, that the level is not likely to drop, leaving you stranded, and that there are no weeds or rubbish floating about to foul your propellers. Move in towards the bank bow first, engine in neutral as you float in, so that the crew member detailed to tie up can just step off onto the bank. On tidal waters, cruisers should come into the mooring against the current and against strong winds, which means you may have to go past your chosen place and turn around.

There may be mooring rings and posts if you are coming onto a regular mooring site, or you may have to use your mooring pins (all hire boats are supplied with these). Mooring lines should be fastened fore and aft of the boat, not at right angles to it, with the bow rope tied up first, and should never be stretched across tow paths for people to trip over. The best mooring places are those on the windward side of the waterway, with the boat's head into the wind.

For sailing craft, the rule is to come into a mooring against the wind, sheets eased. If you have to moor on a leeward bank, lower the sails before drifting slowly into the site.

A busy bank holiday afternoon at Boulters Lock at Maidenhead on the Thames

CHAPTER 6

A Closer Look At Britain's Waterways

The names of waterways in Britain – Severn, Thames and Trent rivers, the Fens, the Broads, canals – have been cropping up throughout this book, and you may wonder why bother to differentiate between them. Surely one body of water is much like another to the holidaymaker? They are, of course, very different both scenically and in what they can offer, and in this chapter I try to pinpoint the differences.

The Broads

The Norfolk Broads, or Broadland, as the area is sometimes called, cover a large part of eastern Norfolk, including Norwich, and extend down into Suffolk near Lowestoft. They comprise a network of waters formed by five rivers: the Ant, Thurne, Bure, Yare and Waveney and their channels and tributaries, interspersed with stretches of water called broads, which look like lakes but which are, in fact, flooded peat diggings cut centuries ago. Only one, Breydon Water, is a true lake. In all, Broadland offers the holidaying boatman 130 miles of navigable waterway (260 miles if he counts it both ways) to explore in any permutation of river, lake, and broad with a dash of seashore. They make easy cruising, too, as there are no locks on Broads rivers and the tide, except at Great Yarmouth, is not difficult.

It is the dash of seashore which does much to make the Broads different from other inland waterways of Britain.

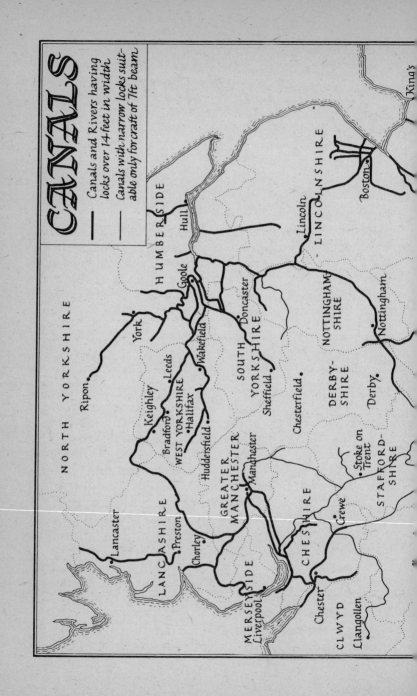

CANALS

— Canals and Rivers having locks over 14 feet in width

— Canals with narrow locks suitable only for craft of 7ft beam

NORTH YORKSHIRE

HUMBERSIDE

LANCASHIRE

WEST YORKSHIRE

GREATER MANCHESTER

SOUTH YORKSHIRE

MERSEYSIDE

CHESHIRE

CLWYD

STAFFORD-SHIRE

DERBY-SHIRE

NOTTINGHAM-SHIRE

LINCOLNSHIRE

Ripon

Lancaster

Preston

Chorley

Liverpool

Chester

Llangollen

Crewe

Stoke on Trent

Derby

Keighley

Bradford

Leeds

Halifax

Huddersfield

Manchester

York

Wakefield

Goole

Hull

Doncaster

Sheffield

Chesterfield

Nottingham

Lincoln

Boston

King's

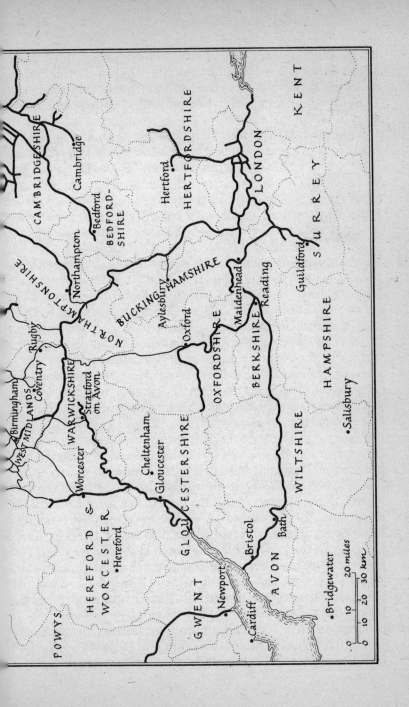

They could have seemed just an area of rather flat, though beautiful, marshy land, but because they are a tidal inlet of the sea, there is an intangible extra something about Broadland air and a delicious whiff of sea breezes to be caught quite far inland.

The sea-tidal nature of the country has also given it other unique features, not least of which is the Norfolk reed which grows in such abundance at the edges of waterways. The reed and the rather brackish water provide a splendid habitat for such a rich variety of wildlife, especially birds, not usually found so far inland, the discovering of which can be one of the greatest pleasures of a Broads holiday.

An important point for skippers to know is that they should not drive their mooring irons into reed banks, as this can destroy the reeds and thus the birds' habitat, and that they should keep clear of shallow waters where fish may spawn. The reed has another use, as thatching for Norfolk buildings, particularly houses and pubs, though it is not unknown on churches. It is harvested early in the year, so holidaymakers may miss this operation, though they are likely to see it set out to dry; they may see sedge, which is also used in the thatching operation, being cut in the summer.

Because the Broads are flat, rather than hilly, they give buildings a great chance to stand out and dominate the landscape. Windmills are splendid landmarks all over the Broads, but particularly along the three northern rivers. Most of them were built to drain the land and their derelict outlines now stand starkly against the sky. Some have been carefully restored and are being lived in, and four – at Berney Arms, Horsey, Sutton and Stracey Arms – are open to the public. (See *Things to see and do* at end of the Broads' section for opening times.) Churches, many of them centuries old and with unusual round towers, give the Broads' landscape another distinctive feature.

The Broads have been a favourite holiday place since the end of Queen Victoria's reign and can still boast the largest boat population anywhere in the British Isles.

About half a million people visit the Broads every year, and some people complain that holidaying there is rather like taking a package holiday in Spain: everywhere is organised, there are people everywhere, so where's the adventure?

It is true that the big agencies have got the hire-boat business almost completely sewn up on the Broads, and to that extent the holidaymaker has little to do beyond reading a brochure or two, choosing his boat and holiday time, paying his money and arriving to take possession of the boat for which he will be solely responsible for the next week or two. But once he has possession, the holidaymaker is on his own and his holiday really can become an adventure. It may be a quiet adventure involving watching at close quarters wildlife which he has never had an opportunity to observe in such detail before, or it may be a jolly romp from pub to pub, taking in the fairgrounds, piers and the seaside pleasures of Great Yarmouth and of Lowestoft, or the theatre, restaurants and discos of Norwich.

Norwich, with its fine cathedral and large outdoor market, is certainly one of the main attractions of the Broads. It has been calculated that nine out of ten of all the holiday boats on the Broads in any one week during summer find their way to the Norwich Yacht Basin. It is a twenty-seven mile trip up the Yare from Great Yarmouth to Norwich, and several stretches have a five-mile an hour speed limit, rather than the standard seven miles, so that there is plenty of time to keep count of the windmills, pubs and other landmarks passed on the way.

Despite the attractions of Norwich, and the commercial traffic which uses it, the Yare, and its sister river, the Waveney, to the south, are rather quieter in the summer than the three northern rivers, the Ant, Thurne and Bure and the Broads associated with them. The largest Broad in the south is Oulton Broad, near Lowestoft, and most of the Broads which attract the holidaymaker, Hickling (which is a nature reserve), Barton, Wroxham, Hoveton, for instance, are all to the north of Norwich.

Each river and its attendant stretches of water have their own characteristics and can offer quite distinct cruises.

The *Ant*, which flows more or less north to south from Wayford Bridge into the Bure at Ludham Bridge west of Horning, is the most northerly reaching of the five rivers. It is narrow and winding and in its upper reaches can seem very remote from civilisation. Perhaps the most interesting thing about it is that it flows right through the large Barton Broad, which is a nature reserve. North of Barton is Sutton Broad which is now little more than a navigation channel, though there is a staithe, a hotel and a village store to serve the holidaymaker. The limits of navigation for larger cruisers on the Ant come shortly after the river forks near Wayford Bridge, one fork becoming the North Walsham and Dilham Canal and the other the Dilham Dyke. These are stretches for small craft only.

Places of interest along the Ant include Irstead, a tiny village with a splendid, thatch-roofed church and a staithe with moorings; Barton Broad which has its own sailing club and a special claim to fame in that Horatio Nelson is thought to have learned to sail there; and Stalham, a market town with its own church, manor house and good selection of shops. There are other small villages down channels or dykes off the main river.

The *Thurne*, like the Ant, flows more or less in a north to south direction, and flows into the Bure at Thurne Mouth. The Thurne's upper reaches have a junction to Hickling Broad, the largest of them all and an important national nature reserve, while the river itself starts life at Martham Broad and West Somerton, which is only about two miles from the coast.

Below Hickling Broad, the Thurne's great claim to fame is the infamous Potter Heigham Bridge, a 700-year-old low-arched structure for which the hire agencies find it worth their while to employ pilots to get their craft through undamaged. Larger craft may have to wait for low tide to pass safely underneath. Potter Heigham itself is an important Broads boat-building centre and is well supplied with shops and pubs.

Downstream is Womack Water, which has a busy staithe, then Thurne, a small village with shop, pub, church and two restored windmills.

The *Bure* is a much longer river than the Ant or the Thurne, meandering from northern Norfolk into the long narrow estuary at Great Yarmouth. It is not navigable for much of its upper reaches, though canoeists can use much of it provided they don't upset the many anglers who also find the Bure north of Coltishall attractive. It is the twenty-nine mile stretch between Great Yarmouth and Coltishall which is of interest to the Broads visitor with a boat, as many of the most attractive Broads, South Walsham, Ranworth, Malthouse and Hoveton Little Broad, lie off this river.

A trip down the river would take in Coltishall, a pleasant village, much of it lying away from the river, and with a good supply of shops and pubs, including two, the Rising Sun and the Anchor Inn, which have riverside moorings.

Wroxham is the next place of any size downstream and is one of the most important places on the Bure. It is among the hire-boat operators' biggest centres on the Broads, and both Blakes and Hoseasons have several yards here, and at Hoveton on the other side of the river. This stretch of the river can get very busy indeed on summer weekends, which adds to the interest of getting through the roadbridge at Wroxham: it is on a bend of the river, which means oncoming boats are difficult to see, and it has a low semi-circular arch to be negotiated as well. Approach with care!

Wroxham Broad, downriver, is the headquarters of the Norfolk Broads Yacht Club, which holds races most weekends in summer.

Further downstream again lies Hoveton Great Broad, which is closed to river traffic, but it is well worth leaving your boat moored at the landing stage while walking round the nature trail which was set up here some years ago by the Nature Conservancy Council.

Salhouse Broad, by contrast, is open and navigable and its lovely setting makes it a popular mooring place.

Hoveton Little Broad is open for navigation but not for fishing, as it is a private Broad and is closed to the public from the middle of September to Spring each year.

The next village to be encountered on a trip downriver is one of the most attractive on the Broads: Horning, with its delightful riverside gardens, well-cared-for inns and staithe.

Just downriver of Horning, to the right lies Cockshoot Dyke and Broad, and further down again another right turning off the river leads to Ranworth and Malthouse Broads. Ranworth is chained off to boats as it is a bird sanctuary and nature reserve owned by the Norfolk Naturalists Trust. It is open to visitors except on Mondays. Ranworth itself boasts one of the finest churches in the whole of Norfolk, and a climb up its tower is rewarded with a splendid view across the surrounding countryside.

Past Ranworth, the Bure continues its leisurely course in wide sweeps past wooded areas into typical Broadland marsh. It passes the entrance to the River Ant, then the remains of the tenth-century monastery and abbey of St Benet where an outdoor church service is held in August each year, conducted by the Bishop of Norwich who comes up river in the Norfolk wherry, the *Albion*.

Then comes Fleet dyke waterway to South Walsham Broad, and the mouth of the River Thurne where a splendidly preserved windmill stands guard.

The stretch of the Bure from Thurne Mouth to Acle Bridge is popular with sailing boats, as it is wide at this point and the winds are usually good for sailing. The Broads which lie to the north of the river below Acle Bridge – Ormesby, Rollesby and Filby – are not accessible by boat, though once there by road, you can hire a rowing boat for bird watching or angling.

On towards Yarmouth, the next village, and the last before Great Yarmouth, is Stokesby which has shops, a pub and moorings. Once the Stracey Arms pub, a mile and a half below Stokesby, is reached, there are no more safe moorings until Yarmouth itself is reached. The river is markedly more tidal than further up, the banks are very reeded, and the river can turn into muddy shallows at low tide. Skippers should take care to keep their boats to the centre of the Bure here, where the depth is usually sufficient, and to watch the marker posts.

Both the other two Broadland rivers, the Yare and the Waveney reach the sea at Great Yarmouth. The Yare, which cuts the Broads roughly in half, flows west to east, directly linking Yarmouth and Norwich, and carries some commercial traffic as well as pleasure craft. Its source can be found at East Dereham, and the twelve-mile stretch from here into Norwich is not navigable. It flows south of the city – the river through the centre of Norwich is the Wensum which joins the Yare at Trowse – and from here on is navigable down to Great Yarmouth. The river is tidal right up to Norwich, where the main mooring site is the Yacht Station on the Wensum, at which mooring fees are charged. Craft coming down river from the Yacht Station pass docks and warehouses, factories, a football club ground (Norwich City FC), and other signs of urban life before the Wensum joins the Yare just past the Trowse railway swing bridge (which does not open for small craft, so yachts must lower their masts).

Thorpe, really a suburb of Norwich, two miles down river, has several agency boatyards and some good moorings. As it is only a short bus ride into Norwich, Thorpe is a useful stopping place for those wishing to avoid the crowded Yacht Basin.

Other villages which make pleasant calling places on the way down river are Brundall, which is a short walk from the river, and Reedham, a pretty village which has achieved some fame through the presence there of Pettitts of Reedham, a firm which began life as a poultry dealer but which now has a thriving feather-craft business. The New Cut, which links the Yare and the Waveney near St Olave's, is entered at Reedham.

The *Yare's* Broads are Surlingham Broad, which is very shallow but has a navigation channel, and which is also a nature reserve owned by the Norfolk Naturalists Trust, and Rockland Broad, another stretch of water liable to silting, so boats must keep within the marked channel. Among the channels and dykes which run off the Yare, the River Chet is the largest. Its junction with the Yare is just upriver from Reedham, and it is navigable for three-and-a-half miles to Loddon, which has boatyards, moorings and shops to attract the holidaymaker.

The last of the Broads' five main rivers is the *Waveney*, which rises between Diss and Thetford, and which is navigable from Geldestone until it joins the Yare at Breydon Water. A branch off it leads to Oulton Broad. Mutford Lock leads from the Broad into Lake Lothing and thence into Lowestoft Harbour, but hire-craft may not proceed beyond the lock: Lowestoft harbour is usually heavy with trawlers, and is no place for a novice boatman.

In its upper limits of navigation the Waveney is particularly lovely. It also feels quite isolated, which gives it an additional attraction for holidaymakers. Villages and towns along the Waveney include Beccles, a splendid old town given its charter by Elizabeth I, which was once a fishing port. It possesses another of those low Broads' bridges which large cruisers may be able to pass under only at low tide; and St Olaves, which has a marina, boatyards, shops and a pub.

Oulton Broad, which is reached from the Waveney via Oulton Dyke, is a very busy Broadland centre, and has good mooring facilities. It is also close to the busy town of Lowestoft, with all its seaside attractions.

Some Notes For Boat Skippers

All the basic rules of the river and sound signals, and other points which everyone in charge of a boat has to bear in mind, apply to boating on the Broads. There are some extra points about the Broads with which you should be fully conversant.

Enjoying a sail in a dinghy on the Broads

All craft, including canoes: must have a *licence* to use the Broads. This is not a problem for people with hire boats, as the operators will have had their boats licenced. Private boat owners and canoeists should apply several weeks in advance of their holiday to obtain a licence. The licencing authority is, The Great Yarmouth Port and Haven Commissioners, 21 South Quay, Great Yarmouth. Tel: Great Yarmouth 55151. The Commissioners also have an office at Carrow Bridge, Norwich. Tel: Norwich 25091.

Cost of the licence will depend on the size of your craft, whether you have a dinghy, and how long you want it for.

Dinghies: are offered as an optional extra by the hire companies, and it is well worth paying the additional hire fee to have one. There are many channels, dykes and creeks which a full-size cruiser could not get into, but which are fun to explore. A dinghy will also enable you to get nearer to the wildlife, and is often essential to get from a mooring place to a pub or village on the other side of the river. You will need a dinghy, too, to fish from in many parts of the Broads.

Navigation: can be a tricky business on the Broads where so many of the waterways are tidal, shallow and lined with marsh and reed. Always keep to the navigation channels, which are clearly marked with posts or marker buoys. Port-hand (left-side going upstream) markers are painted red. Starboard-hand (right-side going upstream) markers are green or black with white tops. A marker post painted black and yellow indicates a fork in the channel. There are special markings on Hickling Broad and Horsey Mere indicating the entrances to Catfield Dyke (off Hickling) and Waxham New Cut (off Horsey). The markings take the form of white posts with white triangles on top. If you get these in line and steer towards them, you will arrive at the Dyke or Cut entrance.

The navigation limits for hire-craft on the Broads are Town Bridge in Great Yarmouth and Mutford Lock on Oulton Broad. And, of course, hire craft may not cruise after dark.

Canoeists are recommended to use the waters beyond the limits of motor navigation, that is, the Bure above Coltishall and the Waveney above Geldeston.

Speed limits: must be carefully observed on the Broads, partly to conserve banks and gardens which can be eroded, and partly to prevent accidents: certain sections of Broadland rivers can get very crowded at the height of summer.

The maximum speed limit over the system is seven miles per hour, but there are also many stretches where the limit is five miles or even three miles per hour. Limits are clearly marked on notices, and the River Commissioners have check points at various places from which they can monitor boats, using stop watches and other devices to measure accurately the speed of craft. They can and do prosecute people flagrantly breaking the limits.

Moorings: are relatively easy to find, except in the more popular towns and villages where places can be full by midday. They are also free in most places except the yacht stations at Beccles, Great Yarmouth, Oulton Broad, and Norwich, Great Yarmouth marina and at Horsey Mere Staithe, Salhouse Broad and Wroxham Broad, and some pubs. People who have hired their boats from a Blakes or Hoseasons boatyard may moor without fee at the agency's other yards.

Remember that the Broad's waters are tidal, and the nearer you moor to the mouths of the Yare, Bure and Waveney, the greater will be the rise and fall of the tide.

Angling On The Broads

Broadland is something of an anglers' paradise with bream, carp, chub, dace, pike, roach, rudd and tench all to be found in the five Broadland rivers, though perhaps less plentifully than used to be the case in the days before large numbers of motor craft made an increase in pollution inevitable.

The authority controlling fishing on the Broads is the

Norfolk and Suffolk Division of the Anglian Water Authority. Their bailiffs patrol the waters of the division regularly, so always have your licence handy.

All fishermen must have a rod licence, issued by the Anglian Water Authority. They can be obtained direct from the Authority, from its local bailiffs or from fishing tackle shops, post offices, some inns, and boatyards. Anglian Water Authority addresses for the Broads are either the head office: Anglian Water Authority, Diploma House, Grammar School Walk, Huntingdon, PE18 6NZ. Tel: Huntingdon 56181; or the relevant divisional office: Anglian Water Authority Norfolk and Suffolk River Division, P.O. Box 50, 62-64 Thorpe Road, Norwich, Norfolk. Tel: Norwich 615161.

You can get a regional licence (£3.85) covering all five divisions of the authority; a divisional licence (£2.00) for one division only; a seven day licence (75p); or a special concessional licence for O.A.P.s, or children aged between twelve and fifteen. The prices quoted are current at the time of publication.

The Water Authority also produces a useful little booklet, *Fishing in Anglia* (25p) which lists the owners of the fishing waters, so that you will know to whom to apply for permits to fish private waters.

Once you have your licence, you can fish on the following waters without a permit: Barton Broad, Decoy Broad, Hickling Broad, Heigham Sound (access only by boat), Little Ormesby, Rollesby, Great Ormesby and Filby Broads (fishing from small dinghies and rowing boats only), Oulton Broad, Salhouse Broad, South Walsham Broad (access only by boat), Surlingham Broad, Womack Water and Wroxham Broad.

The coarse fishing season runs from 15 June through to 15 March.

Among the Water Authority bye-laws, which are exhibited at many points in the Broads, the following are particularly important: Anglers must not leave the keepnet hanging over the side of the boat while it is moving as this kills the fish. Never leave dead fish or other litter lying on river banks. Never throw away lengths of nylon line. These can cause terrible suffering to birds and animals if they get caught up in them. For the same reason, rods should not be left unattended on deck with the line in the water: waterfowl may get entangled in it.

Sailing On The Broads

Sailing is one of the Broads' major attractions, though for the hire-boat holidaymaker, it is an attraction to watch not to take part in, as one of the conditions of hire is that boats may not take part in races. An exception to this rule is Blakes' Barton Regatta Week held at the end of the sailing year, usually in October, in which selected yachts from the Blakes hire fleet may take part. Telephone Blakes at Wroxham 3225 for details of the event and to book your place.

Most regattas on the Broads are club events, though there are some open events, and take place almost every weekend between April and October, with the big regatta weeks being held in August. Two particularly spectacular events in the racing calendar include the Yare Navigation Race for traditional Broads sailing cruisers, which is held towards the end of September, and the Three Rivers Race, one of Britain's major twenty-four hour sailing races covering a fifty-mile course along the Bure, Ant and Thurne, which is held at the end of May.

There are some twenty-five sailing, cruising and yacht clubs based on the Broads, most of which are members of the Norfolk and Suffolk Yachting Association.

Natural History Of The Broads

One of the greatest delights of a Broadland holiday is discovering its natural history, and perhaps recording it with camera or drawing pencil. Many parts of the Broads are nature reserves and access to them is limited or

105

prohibited, but there have been several nature trails established which allow visitors a close look at many aspects of the natural history of the area. It is a good idea to have bird, mammal, plant and insect field guides to hand on the boat. You are likely to catch glimpses of many kinds of creature darting about among the reeds, or flying overhead, as you cruise along, and the books will help settle arguments over whether you have just seen a heron or a great crested grebe, a coypu or a water rat.

Nature Reserves And Trails On The Broads

Barton Broad: a reserve belonging to the Norfolk Naturalists Trust, and has the River Ant flowing through it. Herons may often be seen here as there is a heronry nearby, and the great crested grebe nests on the Broad itself. Other birds to watch out for include the ubiquitous mallard duck, teal, grey lag geese, Canada geese, bitterns and black terns.

Breydon Water: has public footpaths along the north and south banks coming away from Great Yarmouth and Gorleston. Wading birds may be seen in good numbers on the mud flats.

Cockshoot and Ranworth Broads: lie off the Bure downstream of Horning. Like Barton Broad, these two belong to the Norfolk Naturalists Trust and are part of the Bure Marshes National Nature Reserve. They provide a safe habitat for many species of wildfowl, who winter on its waters. The Broadland Conservation Centre at Ranworth is a floating building with a gallery from which the birds may be viewed. Open April to October, daily except Mondays and Saturday mornings.

Hickling Broad National Nature Reserve: another area in the care of the Norfolk Naturalists Trust. This is a particularly important nature reserve, and boats are strictly controlled both in numbers and in where they may go. There are limited mooring facilities, and a carefully marked channel across the centre of the Broad.

There are facilities for serious naturalists to join small boat or trail walking parties and to visit several hides. There is also a Water Trail organised in summer, from June until mid-September, on Tuesdays, Wednesdays and Thursdays, for which advance booking is essential. Applications for permits and tickets for the Water Trail should be made to the Warden, Warden's Office, Stubb Road, Hickling, Norwich, NR12 0BW. Tel: Hickling 276.

Hoveton Great Broad Nature Trail: is on the privately owned Hoveton Broad, now part of the Bure Marshes National Nature Reserve. Boats cannot cruise on the Broad, but the Nature Conservancy Council has established a splendid nature trail which allows visitors to see examples of the vegetation and land which make up the fenland ecology. You cannot get to the Broad by land, only by boat along the Bure. There is a quay on the north bank upstream of the entrance to Salhouse Broad. The Hoveton Broad Nature Trail is usually open Monday to Friday, 10 am to 5.30 pm from early May until mid-September. There is an admission charge for adults, and children under sixteen get in free.

Lion Wood: run by the City of Norwich Amenities Department, is a trail through one mile of woodland in Woodrow Pilling Park, Harvey Lane, Norwich. It is open all year.

Strumpshal Fen (RSPB) near Norwich: is a small Broad with reed beds and mixed woodland. A public hide has been set up near Buckenham for views of wintering birds, and there is a nature trail. People wishing to visit should contact the Warden, Tel: Norwich 715191.

Surlingham Broad Nature Reserve: is a Norfolk Naturalists Trust reserve not open to the general public, and is certainly not open to boats, as the Broad has, over the years, dwindled away into a few drainage channels and very shallow water covered with dense carpets of vegetation. The vegetation is of considerable interest to the naturalist, and many kinds of wildfowl and wading birds also visit it. Anyone wishing to visit the reserve must contact the Honorary Warden, Dr E.A. Ellis, Wheatfen

Broad, Surlingham, Norwich. Tel: Surlingham 239.

Other Things To See And Do In Broadland

The Broads are particularly attractive for a family boating holiday because there are so many things to see and do, and many places to visit within easy reach of most of the public mooring places.

Obvious attractions are Norwich, Great Yarmouth and Lowestoft, each with public moorings within walking distance and all of them with many things, including museums, galleries, live entertainment, restaurants, discos, cinemas and good shopping, to interest the holiday-maker.

The tourist information centres in each town can send you booklets and pamphlets listing attractions, with opening times, admission fees etc. Addresses are:

Great Yarmouth: Department of Publicity and Attractions, 14 Regent Street. Tel: Great Yarmouth 4313. Information Bureau, Marine Parade. Tel: Great Yarmouth 2195. (This office is open only in the summer.)

Lowestoft: Information Bureau, The Esplanade. Tel: Lowestoft 65989.

Norwich: Tourist Information Centre, Augustine Steward House, 14 Tombland. Tel: Norwich 23445/20679.

For East Anglia generally: The East Anglia Tourist Board, 14 Museum Street, Ipswich IP1 1HU. Tel: Ipswich 214211

The Board can send you pamphlets and booklets listing many kinds of attractions – museums, galleries, transport collections, castles, stately homes, nature reserves and nature trails – all over their area, including opening times and prices.

Finally, because windmills are such a feature of the Broads, a few which welcome visitors, are:

Berney Arms Mill: on the west bank of the Yare, four-and-a-quarter miles upriver from Great Yarmouth and six miles south of Acle, off the B1140. This mill, which includes a small museum, was built as a drainage mill in about 1860. Its tower is 70 feet high. Open April to September, 9.30 am to 7 pm.

Horsey Mill (National Trust): a fine example of a Broads drainage wind pump at Horsey Mere staithe, by the B1159. Open during daylight hours in summer.

Stracey Arms Windmill: on the south bank of the Bure, downriver from Stokesby. A drainage mill, and a fine landmark as well. Open from May to September, daily, 9 am to 5 pm.

Sutton Windmill: off the A149 near Stalham. This enormous corn windmill, the tallest in the country, is privately owned and is still being restored. Open April to September, daily, 9.30 am to 6 pm. Tel: Stalham 81195 for booking parties.

The Fens (map 4)

The Fenlands of England are an area west and south of the Wash, south of Lincoln to Suffolk. Centuries ago they were swampland, covered in marsh and reed and almost uninhabited. The Romans tried to drain the western edges of the Fens when they dug Caer Dyke, traces of which can still be found, but in Anglo-Saxon times the land was a buffer between different tribes. Hereward the Wake made the last stand of the Anglo-Saxons against William the Conqueror at Ely in the Fens in 1071.

The great drainage schemes which began in the seventeenth century, and which have continued into the twentieth, have transformed this swampland into very rich farming land indeed, giving it a character quite different from other British inland waterways. The manmade waterways were built for drainage purposes, and draining the land is still their main function today. Some of them have been cut straight across the land, rather like a watery Roman road. Their locks are vast and solid, and heavy to operate; they need to be to withstand the pressures of huge quantities of water that at certain times of the year may come rushing down the rivers and channels.

The Fens' waterways are a very pleasant place indeed on which to spend a cruising holiday, as more and more people have been discovering in recent years. They are quiet, much quieter than the Broads, despite the fact that two of the booking agencies now have boatyard connections there to deal with increased demand, and in many places they seem very remote from the hurly-burly and tensions of city life. The skies above are wide and empty, though you may see great flocks of birds such as geese, or a flight of half a dozen ducks, passing overhead. The horizon seems to stretch into infinity over fields which you may find yourself looking down on from your boat, as subsidence has left the water navigations higher than the surrounding countryside along several stretches.

There are many attractive towns on or near the Fens' waterways, including Earith, Hemingford, Huntingdon, Godmanchester and St Neots on the Ouse; two superb cathedrals, at Ely and Peterborough, and the university city of Cambridge. The Fens have their fair share of welcoming pubs, though in keeping with the quiet feel of the area, most of them are not built on the water's edge, but have to be approached on foot from your mooring. The Fenlands boast a good collection of stately homes, museums, nature reserves and other attractions, too, which add extra enjoyment to a family holiday. Real waterway enthusiasts would not dream of going to the Fens without having a good look at the famous pumping engine at Stretham on the Old West River.

The Fenlands' drainage system is based on two main rivers, the Nene and the Great Ouse and their tributaries, including the Cam, the Lark, the Little Ouse and the Wissey, and on a series of canals and navigations roughly ninety-two miles long called the Middle Level Navigations. These connect the Great Ouse and the Nene, so that it is not necessary for boats to make the difficult passage across the Wash, with its shallows, mists and difficult tides, to get from one river to the other. The key to the whole drainage system is the larger Denver Sluice near Downham Market, which is the limit of navigation for hire-craft.

Sometimes the Nene and the Middle Level Navigations have to be closed to navigation if heavy rain has caused flooding and the locks have to be opened to allow the water to pass. This happened at the height of the holiday season in 1980, and it is a possible drawback to planning a holiday on the Fens' waterways. But it does not happen very often, and when it does it is usually in winter.

As with other waterway systems, craft have to be registered to operate on the Nene and the Great Ouse and their tributaries. In 1980 the Anglian Waterway Authority, the authority for most of the Fens' waterways, introduced a new system for issuing registration and navigation licences. There were quite a few 'ifs' and 'buts' about the system, which had not been sorted out by the time this book went to press, so I cannot tell you exactly what you will need and what it is likely to cost you in 1981. Roughly, the system requires all boats to be registered and to display a registration disc. Boat skippers also have to pay a navigation fee. Costs for these depends on the length of the boat, the horsepower of its engine, the length of time you want to be registered for, and for which rivers.

Holidaymakers wishing to cruise on both the Nene and the Great Ouse can pay one set of registration and navigation fees to cover both. This regional fee is, of course, more expensive than the restricted fee allowing navigation on just one river.

A further complication in 1980 was that two fees were available – an annual fee and a twenty-eight day fee, but the latter was only available to people who already had a British Waterways Board licence for the canal system.

People wishing to cruise on the Nene and to go through its locks also have to hire a special lock key, for which there is a refundable security deposit.

In 1980, the Anglian Water Authority found that many

111

hire boat operators were sending their customers direct to the Authority to get their fees and keys. Boat operators could do the registering themselves and also obtain keys for their customers, and it may well be that in 1981 they will administer this matter.

Once you have decided which Fens' waterways you want to cruise on, you should get in touch with the relevant authorities for up-to-date information.

For the River Nene: The Anglian Water Authority, Welland & Nene Rivers Division, North Street, Oundle, Peterborough, PE8 4AS. Tel: Oundle 3701.

For the River Great Ouse, its tributaries, and the Cam below Bottisham Lock: The Anglian Water Authority, Great Ouse River Division, Great Ouse House, Clarendon Road, Cambridge, CB2 2BL. Tel: Cambridge 61561.

For the Cam above Bottisham Lock: The River Cam Conservancy, The Guildhall, Cambridge, CB2 3QT. Tel: Cambridge 58977.

For the Middle Level Navigations: Middle Level Commissioners, Dartford Street, March, Cambs, PE15 8AF. Tel: March 3232.

If you are doing your own registering, you should get in touch with the Anglian Water Authority ten to fourteen working days in advance of the date of your holiday.

You do not have to pay licence fees or toll charges on the Middle Level Navigations, but it is always wise to write to the commissioners a couple of weeks in advance of your holiday to get up-to-date reports on locks, weed growth (which can be heavy and has to be cut), etc. You must also give them forty-eight hours' notice of your intention of locking through the Stanground Sluice near Peterborough; it may be necessary for them to adjust the water levels and, more important, the lock-keeper is a working farmer who cannot leave his farm at a moment's notice. The length of the Stanground Sluice is 49 feet, thus limiting the length of boats which can pass through it to about 46 feet. Wide-beam craft more than 40 feet long also could not negotiate the sharp bend through Briggate, Whittlesey.

The *River Nene*, which is navigable for about ninety miles and has thirty-eight locks along its length, traces a course from Northampton to the Wash. In its upper reaches between Northampton and Peterborough, it flows through the lovely Nene Valley. Below the curiously named 'Dog-in-a-Doublet' lock with its waterside inn of the same name, which lies some five miles downstream of Peterborough, the river is tidal and hire-craft may not pass beyond the lock.

The Nene's locks, which require special keys, obtainable from the Anglian Waterways Authority, are famous for their guillotine bottom lock gates which pull up and down, rather than opening and closing like most other canal locks.

The special key unlocks the large fixed handle which winds the lock's lower guillotine gates; the usual windlass unlocks the top gates. Always leave the bottom guillotine gates open when you have locked through.

The narrowest lock on the Nene will take craft with a 13-foot beam, though if you are coming onto the Nene from the Grand Union Canal's Northampton arm, you will be in a narrow beam craft, anyway, because of the latter's 7-foot locks.

The Nene is a delightful river for cruising. It's winding and pretty, with water mills, church towers and charming villages breaking the long line of the horizon. Two stately homes, Castle Ashby and Elton Hall, are within easy reach of the river, as are the remains of Fotheringhay Castle where Mary, Queen of Scots was executed. Northampton and Peterborough, both manufacturing towns, are interesting to visit, Peterborough in particular, making the boating fraternity welcome with a fine stretch of moorings. It is an easy walk from the river up Bridge Street to Peterborough's superb cathedral, begun in 1118.

It is possible to get from the mouth of the Nene to the mouth of the Great Ouse across the Wash, but this is a trip for experienced boatmen only. The Wash at this point has many shallows, tides and currents are strong, and mists often come down without warning. Many cruisers, including hire-cruisers which cannot go much further downstream anyway, leave the Nene at the Stanground Sluice and make for the Great Ouse via the *Middle Level Navigations*.

The Navigations lead, via several different routes, to the Great Ouse near Denver Sluice. Their total length is about ninety-two miles, with four locks, but the best route between the two rivers is about thirty miles. The route recommended is via the Whittlesey Dyke and March on the Old River Nene, up to Well Creek and so into the Great Ouse at Salter's Lode Lock. The Middle Level Commissioners recommend this route because erosion of the banks and shallows make navigation difficult on other watercourses. They can send a map, plus notes of the route (lock diversions, names and addresses of lock-keepers etc.) to anyone intending to use the Navigations as a passage between the two rivers. Navigation is prohibited in the Middle Level Main Drain between St Germans and the aqueduct.

Nine out of ten boats using the Middle Level Navigations do so to get from one river to the other; they are less attractive than the Nene and the Great Ouse as cruising waterways, partly because they are deep drainage navigations so that boats travel many miles between high banks with restricted views of the countryside. They are a fisherman's paradise, however, providing some of the best coarse fishing in the country, and match fishing takes place during most weekends in the season. In fact, a good part of the Middle Level Commissioners' income derives from the letting of fishing rights.

The *Great Ouse* is the biggest of the Fenland rivers; its head of navigation is Castle Mill Lock at Bedford, and it flows into the Wash near King's Lynn, a distance of some seventy-five miles. There are seventeen locks, and the river has junctions with the Cam, the Lark, Little Ouse and Wissey, as well as the Middle Level Navigations.

The Great Ouse is a lovely river – 'a classic among English rivers' it has been called, and with reason. In its upper levels it follows a winding course, lined with trees, fields and fine old villages, including Eaton Socon, St Neots, Godmanchester and Huntingdon, where Oliver Cromwell was born, and Hemingford Grey, an exceptionally attractive village, with the last un-manned lock on the Ouse; below here there are lock-keepers to assist you. There are many interesting old bridges on the river but none more so than the St Ives chapel bridge (there is a tiny chapel in the centre of the bridge).

At Earith Junction, the waterway enters the Old West River, flowing slightly east then north, while the Old Bedford River branches off to the Denver Sluice. A fascinating curiosity on the Old West River is the Stretham pumping engine, with its steam machinery dating back to 1831; the engine house is open to the public.

Downriver from Pope's Corner, the junction with the Cam, the river broadens and the land is true Fen – flat and undulating. Above it, the great tower of Ely Cathedral stands clear and isolated on the horizon.

On the sixteen-mile stretch of the river from Ely downriver to the Denver Sluice, there are several small rivers branching off, offering good stretches of delightful cruising.

The *River Lark*, which is navigable for nearly thirteen miles to Jude's Ferry. There is one lock, at Isleham.

The *Little Ouse*, which is navigable for thirteen miles until it reaches a series of disused locks at Brandon.

The *River Wissey* which has a ten mile navigable stretch from the Great Ouse to Stoke Ferry.

The *River Cam* qualifies as a river in its own right, rather than just a branch of the Great Ouse. It is just over fourteen miles long, from Cambridge to Pope's Corner near Ely, has three manned locks with picturesque names, Jesus, Baits Bite and Bottisham, and several navigable navigation channels called the Cambridgeshire Lodes. Burwell Lode, entered via Upware Lock, leads to the National Trust's Wicken Fen, which is very rich in plant

115

and insect life and a good variety of birds.

Angling In The Fens

A rod licence, issued by the Anglian Water Authority, Fisheries Department, and obtainable from the authority and its bailiffs, or from fishing tackle shops, is needed to fish the Fen rivers and navigations. The same licences are available as for the Broads (see page 103) which are also a division of the Anglian Water Authority.

Permits are also needed to fish waters owned or leased by clubs and other organisations or individuals. The local inn or tackle shop will be able to tell you who owns what, or you can get from the Anglian Water Authority a copy of their book *Fishing in Anglia* (25p).

The Water Authority's fishing officers and the Middle Level Commissioners are concerned that fishermen should not be disturbed by inconsiderate cruiser skippers. Remember always to keep your speed down when passing fishermen, and give them a wide berth so that you do not foul their lines.

Finding The Tourist Attractions

The tourist board covering the Fens is The East Anglia Tourist Board, 14 Museum Street, Ipswich, Suffolk. Tel: Ipswich 2 14211. The Board produces several useful publications and maps to help the visitor find places of interest. The *East Anglia Guide* includes a map of the area and has detailed lists of historic trails, restaurants etc. giving opening times and prices.

Other tourist information offices in the Fens area are:
Cambridge: Tourist Information Centre, Wheeler Street, Cambridge. Tel: Cambridge 358977.
Ely: Tourist Information Centre, Town Hall, Bridge Street, Peterborough. Tel: Peterborough 63141.

The English And Welsh Canals

In this section I give a profile of each navigable pleasure canal, including where it is, how long it is and how many locks will be encountered along it. I list the authority which supervises it and give a note of its particular attractions. Where the note says a canal is 'broad' I mean that its locks will take wide-beam craft; a 'narrow' canal means one on which the locks are 7 feet wide.

The British Waterways Board is the authority responsible for the great majority of the English, Welsh and Scottish canals, and other inland waterways; some 2000 miles in all, situated as far north as Inverness and as far south as Somerset. There are various aspects of the Board's work which those responsible for pleasure boats should know about if they are to get the maximum pleasure and enjoyment from their canal holiday.

Licences

Every pleasure boat including a canoe or kayak, has to have a licence (for waterways) or a River Registration Certificate (for river navigations).

People hiring a boat do not need to worry about these, as the hire-boat operator obtains them. Owners of private craft can get licence and registration forms from, and pay the fees to, The Craft Licensing Supervisor, British Waterways Board, Willow Grange, Church Road, Watford, WD1 3QA. Tel: Watford 26422. Licences are issued for one, three, six, or twelve months, and must be prominently displayed on the boat for which they are obtained. Cost depends on various factors, including size, horsepower of engines etc. When applying for a licence, allow plenty of time for the Supervisor's office to handle the paperwork as they get a large number of applications every year.

Licences for canals not under the Board's supervision, or not having a reciprocal agreement with the Board, have to be obtained from the relevant authority; their addresses are given in the notes for the canals.

Moorings

The Board have established mooring sites throughout the waterway system, and many others are provided by boatyards, clubs and local authority marinas. Towpath mooring is permitted almost everywhere (exceptions are sign-posted) and most mooring to the Board's land is free of charge for up to fourteen consecutive days in any two-month period.

Preserving The Canals (area offices):

Canals require constant vigilance to keep them in good repair. Although the British Waterways Board employ engineers and supervisors to watch over the whole system and make repairs as quickly as possible, they can't be everywhere at once, and to a certain extent rely on the public informing them of damaged banks, leaks and floodings. If you do see any signs of these, or if you see anyone vandalising locks and towpaths, you should report the matter to the nearest area engineer as soon as possible. A leaking or collapsed bank ignored could mean miles of unnavigable waterway.

The area offices and their addresses are:

Wigan: Swan Meadow Road, Wigan, Greater Manchester, WN3 5BB. Tel: Wigan 42239.

Castleford: Lock Lane, Castleford, West Yorks, WF10 2LH. Tel: Castleford 554351.

Northwich: Navigation Road, Northwich, Cheshire. Tel: Northwich 74321.

Nottingham: 24 Meadow Lane, Nottingham, NG2 3HL. Tel: Nottingham 862411.

Birmingham: Reservoir House, Icknield Port Road, Birmingham, B16 0AA. Tel: 021 454 7091.

Gloucester: Dock Office, Gloucester, GL1 2EJ. Tel: Gloucester 25524.

London: 43 Clarendon Road, Watford, WD1 1JE. Tel: Watford 31363.

Stoppages (Canalphone):

It is necessary from time to time to close canals to all craft while repair and maintenance work is carried out. Most 'stoppages' as they are called, are planned well in advance and you can take them into account when planning a holiday. The area offices listed above can tell you about planned stoppages.

To find out about unplanned stoppages, caused perhaps by flooding or accidents, telephone the Board's *Canalphone* recorded answering service, a three minute tape of information about unscheduled stoppages. For unscheduled stoppages *north* of Worcester on the Worcester and Birmingham Canal, Napton Junction on the Oxford Canal and Norton Junction on the Grand Union Canal, telephone 01 723 8486. For unscheduled stoppages *south* of Autherley Junction on the Shropshire Union Canal, Fradley Junction on the Trent and Mersey Canal and Trent Junction on the River Soar, telephone 01 723 8487.

Observing The Bye-laws

Most of the British Waterways Board's bye-laws which pleasure boat skippers should know about have been covered in Chapter 5, but there are a few others relevant to pleasure boats and their crews using the canals.

Bye-law 15, for instance, says that 'no person shall use any pole, boat hook or other instrument in such a manner as to cause injury to any person or damage to any property'.

Bye-law 19 covers the navigation of pleasure craft: 'A pleasure boat when meeting, overtaking or being over-

Push-tow craft typical of modern commercial users of the canals at work in the north east

taken by a power-driven vessel other than a pleasure boat shall as far as possible keep out of the main navigable channel. . . . When two pleasure boats, one of which is a sailing vessel are proceeding in such directions as to involve risk of collision, the pleasure boat not being a sailing vessel shall keep out of the way of the sailing vessel'.

Bye-law 27 forbids people, animals and vehicles remaining on moveable bridges once warning has been given that the bridge is about to be opened.

The throwing of rubbish, stones or other material into the canals is prohibited (Bye-law 40).

Swimming is prohibited in the Board's canals, (Bye-law 41), as is water-skiing without the Board's express consent.

Finally, Bye-law 52: 'The master of any vessel using any canal shall be responsible for the safety and security of the vessel and its moorings and shall be answerable to the Board for any damage done by such vehicle employed about the same to the canal, vessels, goods and property of the Board in or on any part of the canal'.

The Board's bye-laws are enforced by Patrol Superintendents and Patrol Officers, who may prosecute anyone breaking them. They use stop-watches and other devices in their patrol launches to check the speed of craft and can come down very heavily on anyone breaking the speed limit – four miles per hour on most canals.

Angling On The Canals

Angling is one of the most popular leisure pursuits connected with the canals, with about a quarter of a million people using the Board's canals and reservoirs every year. Most of the fishing rights have been leased to clubs and associations (a list of which may be found in the *Waterways Companion*), but some fisheries are directly controlled by the Board.

Every fisherman must have a rod licence, issued by the regional water authorities, and obtainable either from

121

the relevant authority or from local fishing tackle shops. Day permits are also needed for fishing waters leased out to clubs, but these can usually be obtained on the spot from patrolling bailiffs as required.

The British Waterways Board's Fisheries Officer can be contacted at Willow Grange, Church Road, Watford, WD1 3QA.

The Canals

The following is a list of the main pleasure craft canals in England and Wales. Several of these canals can be navigated in a 'ring' so that you can arrive back at your starting point without having gone back on your tracks. There are two rings very popular with holidaymakers, each one slightly less than a hundred miles long, and needing two weeks to cruise in comfort.

The Cheshire Ring: Macclesfield, Rochdale, Peak Forest, Ashton, Bridgewater, Trent and Mersey Canals.

The Avon Ring: the river Avon and the Stratford and Birmingham and Worcester Canals.

Aire And Calder Navigation (map 9):

a broad canal, from the docks at Goole on the Yorkshire Ouse to Leeds: Length, 34 miles. Locks: 13. Authority, British Waterways Board

This is a busy commercial canal though pleasure craft use it too, partly because it links up with several canal systems, and partly because the commercial traffic gives it a special interest. This is the canal on which to look out for 'Tom Puddings' (trains of square, coal-carrying compartment boats), oil tanker barges, and British Waterways tugs, among other commercial craft. Much of the canal winds through industrial areas, passing several power stations, including the Ferrybridge Complex, giving the holidaymaker a chance to see Britain at work from a new angle, but parts of it also cut through some fine countryside.

In the busy commercial sections, holiday boats should give way to commercial traffic, keeping a watch for long trains of barges, especially on bends.

There are two branches off the Aire and Calder: from Castleford to Wakefield, seven-and-a-half miles long, with four locks, linking the main Navigation with the Calder and Hebble Navigation; from Knottingley (the Bank Dole junction) to Selby, eleven-and-three-quarter miles long, with four locks, a link to the Yorkshire Ouse.

At its Leeds end, the Aire and Calder links up with the Leeds and Liverpool Canal via the River Aire. It is also connected with the Sheffield and South Yorkshire Canal via the New Junction Canal.

Ashby Canal (map 5):

a narrow canal, from Marston Junction near Bedworth on the Coventry Canal to Snarestone: Length: 22 miles. Locks: 1 (the Marston Junction stop lock; the canal itself has no locks). Authority: British Waterways Board.

A trip on this canal could well turn the novice canaller into an enthusiast for life. It is not long but it passes through an attractive countryside of farms and woods, and there are no locks, so it is a good canal for a beginner. On the other hand, it has two aqueducts and a tunnel (the 250-yard Snarestone tunnel) to add some excitement to the cruising. The canal passes within a mile of the site of the Battle of Bosworth Field, where Richard III was killed in 1485, and the Tudors, in the person of Henry VII, snatched the crown of England from under a thorn bush, or so the story goes. There are also a number of attractive pubs, an important factor in the making of a canal enthusiast.

Once a very important coal-carrying canal, the Ashby now stops a mile past the Snarestone tunnel. Beyond here stretches of the canal have subsided, because of mining works, and have been filled in.

Ashton Canal (map 10):

a narrow canal, from the junction with the Rochdale
Canal in Manchester to the junction with the Peak Forest
Canal at Dukinfield, Ashton-under-Lyne. Length: 6¼
miles. Locks: 18. Authority: British Waterways Board.

This canal, dug in the 1790s, was re-opened as recently
as 1974 after a great voluntary clearance scheme. It runs
through urban Manchester, and its importance lies in the
fact that it is a vital link in the Cheshire Ring. Its eighteen
locks, which need a special key to unlock the paddle gear
(because of vandalism: arrange for the key in advance
with your hire company or the British Waterways Board),
make this short canal slow going. Experienced users of
the canal recommend that you lock up your boat if you
leave it to go shopping in Manchester's Piccadilly area.

Basingstoke Canal (map 1):

a narrow canal, from Byfleet on the River Wey in Surrey
to Basingstoke in Hampshire. Length: 32 miles. Locks:
29. Authorities: River Wey to Aldershot, Surrey County
Council. Aldershot to Odiham, Hampshire County Council.

This canal is not navigable at present, but a great deal of
work by volunteers and members of government Job
Creation schemes in the late 1970s has raised hopes that it
will be open to pleasure craft in the mid-1980s.

Birmingham Canal Navigations (map 5):

a network of narrow canals, cut across an area of the
Midlands roughly bound by Birmingham in the south-
east and, in a roughly clockwise direction, Stourbridge,
Dudley, Wolverhampton, Walsall and Rushall. Length:
Over 100 miles. Locks: 200. Authority: British Waterways
Board.

Just as Birmingham has its Spaghetti Junction of roads,
so it has a positive spaghetti bowlful of canals.

Suffice it to say that the BCN consists of a fifteen-and-a-half mile main line, from Worcester Bar near the centre of Birmingham to Aldersley Junction near Wolverhampton, seventeen major branches (some of which are closed) and twenty-five minor branches (many of which are closed).

The whole system is a joy to connoisseurs: something to get their teeth into for months, even years, as they trace the line of James Brindley's original cut, a contour canal, because the area was hilly and lacked plentiful water supplies, or note Thomas Telford's improvements, admire some fine iron bridges, or leg their boat through the Dudley Tunnel. (Boats must be legged or pushed through the tunnel because the ventilation is insufficient to deal with engine fumes.)

Contrary to what you might think, the BCN has long stretches of open countryside to offer, and not too much grey and dirty industrial water to concern the holidaymaker. The system well repays a close look.

Bridgewater Canal (map 10):

a broad canal from the junction with the Rochdale Canal at Castleford, Manchester, to the junction with the Manchester Ship Canal in Manchester. Length: 28 miles. Locks: none (but Hulme Lock connects a short branch of the canal with the Manchester Ship Canal). Authority: Manchester Ship Canal Co., (Bridgewater Transport Services), Trafford Road, Manchester. Tel: 061 872 7031.

Historically, this is one of the most important canals on the English and Welsh canal system, for it, or at least its branch from Stretford to Leigh, was the canal which got the whole canal boom going in the late eighteenth century. The canal now forms part of the Cheshire Ring.

The canal's branches are: Stretford (near Manchester) to Leigh Junction with a branch of the Leeds and Liverpool Canal, 10¾ miles; Preston Brook branch, from Waters Meeting to the Preston Brook junction with the Trent and Mersey Canal, ¾ mile; Hulme Locks branch from

Egerton Street Bridge, Manchester to the Manchester Ship Canal (River Irwell Upper Reach), ⅜ mile.

On the Stretford-Leigh branch is the 235 feet long Barton Swing Aqueduct, which pivots open to allow ships to pass beneath, with great steel gates holding the water in both the canal and the aqueduct. And, no, you and your boat may not stay in the aqueduct as it swings open and shut.

Holidaymakers should note that the Barton Swing Aqueduct has to be closed for two or three weeks (usually at the end of September/beginning of October) every year for overhaul. To check that this closure does not coincide with your holiday, telephone the above number.

Calder And Hebble Navigation (map 9):

a broad canal from the junction with the Aire and Calder Canal at Wakefield to Sowerby Bridge in Yorkshire. Length: 21½ miles. Locks: 39 (including several flood locks). Authority: British Waterways Board.

A part-canal, part-river navigation which is not as surrounded by the sights and sounds of industry as you might think from its location. Once past Mirfield, stretches of it display some very fine scenery and there are plenty of trees edging the towpath.

An interesting oddity of this canal is the fact that you have to have a handspike rather than the usual windlass to operate the lock paddles above Brighouse. You can borrow these from the British Waterways Board yard at Shepley Bridge and Castleford.

The major part of this canal, from Broadcut Top Lock to Sowerby Bridge, has locks which will not take craft longer than 57 ft 6 in.

Chesterfield Canal (map 9):

a mainly narrow canal, from the junction with the River Trent at West Stockwith north of Gainsborough to Worksop. (The canal is largely unnavigable from Worksop to Chesterfield.) Length: 26 miles. Locks: 16. Authority: British Waterways Board.

Although it now seems just a very pretty country canal, the Chesterfield once carried a lot of freight: coal, timber, grain and stone as well as domestic goods, as it was an important highway in the late eighteenth century before roads were built in the area. There is a 154-yard tunnel at Drakeholes and an aqueduct at Retford, which is the limit of navigation for broad-beam cruisers. Above this point, locks become 7 feet wide.

There is only one entrance to the Chesterfield Canal, and that is via the tidal Trent, which can be awkward, partly because of the tide and partly because there is an aegre on the Trent. Always get lock-keepers' advice before tackling the canal entrance.

Coventry Canal (map 5):

a narrow canal from the junction with the Oxford Canal at Hawkesbury Junction near Coventry to the junction with the Trent and Mersey Canal at Fradley. Length: 32½ miles. Locks: 13. Authority: British Waterways Board.

As might be expected from its location, this canal shows many contrasts between the industrial and the rural. It's a useful canal to use to by-pass Birmingham, and the presence of Coventry and its magnificent post-war cathedral at the end of a branch of the canal.

The canal has a junction with the Ashby Canal at Marston, three miles north of Hawkesbury, and a junction with the Wyrley and Essington Canal at Huddlesford.

Erewash Canal (the Grand Union Canal) (map 9):

a broad canal from the River Trent near Sawley, Notts, to Langley Mill. Length: 12 miles. Locks: 15. Authority: British Waterways Board.

A canal within the Grand Union Canal system, the Erewash passes through a largely industrial area, interspersed with some green sections. The Great Northern

Basin, restored in recent years with much volunteer labour, is an excellent one. It marks the end of navigation on this part of the canal system, because the Cromford Canal, whose junction is at this point, is now derelict.

Exeter Ship Canal:

a broad canal from Turf Lock on the River Exe estuary to Exeter, Devon. Length: 5 miles, 1½ furlongs. Locks: 1. Authority: The Corporation of the City of Exeter, Municipal Offices, Exeter. Harbourmaster and canal superintendent, tel: Exeter 74306.

Until the early 1970s this historic canal was busy with commercial shipping. Today, it is very quiet with just the ferry from Exmouth and some pleasure craft using it. The building of the M5 motorway over the canal reduced its height to ten metres, thus preventing large commercial craft using it; yachts usually take their masts down at Turf Lock. It is off the hire-boat routes, of course, but private craft may still explore it, or use it for winter laying-up. The side lock at Topsham into the River Exe is dilapidated and in need of renovation. Locking, assistance and laying-up fees are all payable at the Exeter Municipal Offices.

Fossdyke Canal (map 8):

a broad canal, from the River Trent at Torksey to the River Witham at High Bridge, Lincoln. Length: 11¼ miles. Locks: 1. Authority: British Waterways Board.

This broad navigation was dug by the Romans in the second century AD, partly to move grain and partly for drainage. Henry I deepened it in 1121. It is still a fairly busy waterway today, and places well worth visiting include the village of Saxilby and Lincoln, whose superb medieval cathedral stands on a hill above the town.

The Fossdyke is entered from the tidal Trent via Torksey Lock, and boats arriving to lock in at low tide may find they have to wait for several hours for the tide to make a level.

Gloucester And Sharpness Ship Canal (map 7):

a broad canal, from Gloucester to Sharpness, Gloucestershire. Length: 16¾ miles. Locks: 2 (one at each end).
Authority: British Waterways Board.

This canal, not much used by holidaymakers, by-passes
the difficult stretch of the River Severn between Gloucester and Sharpness. The canal has its own difficulties for
the inexperienced: it is used by larger commercial shipping,
and the entrance channel at Gloucester has a swift
current. On the other hand, the canal passes through
some very lovely scenery and there are several welcoming
pubs en route.

Grand Union Canal (maps 2 and 5):

a mainly broad canal, but with narrow sections, from the
Thames in London to Birmingham and Leicester. Length:
Main line – 135 miles, Leicester Section – 78 miles. Locks:
Main line – 165, Leicester Section – 59. Authority:
British Waterways Board.

The Grand Union Canal is Britain's longest canal,
though it is not really one canal at all. It was formed
initially in 1929 by an amalgamation of two major canals,
the Grand Junction and the London and Leicester Canals,
to which others were added in 1932, when the vast system
became known as the Grand Union Canal.

The Main Line, the London to Norton Junction stretch
and then on to Birmingham, is a popular one with
holidaymakers as it passes through many interesting and
very beautiful areas, not least of which is its beginning at
Brentford near Kew on the Thames, on its way via the
Chilterns through the heart of England. It is also well
supplied with boatyards, chandlers, moorings and marinas,
which adds to the comfort of the journey.

Navigable branches of the Main Line are the Regent's
Canal from Limehouse Basin to Paddington (see separate
entry); Slough Arm, nearly five miles long, from nine
miles above Brentford to Slough in Berkshire; Wendover

Arm from lock 45 on the Main Line to Tring, one-and-a-half miles; Aylesbury Arm, a narrow canal, six-and-a-quarter miles long, from Marsworth junction to Aylesbury, Buckinghamshire; Northampton Arm, a narrow canal, four-and-three-quarter miles long, from the junction at Gayton on the Main Line to the junction with the River Nene at Northampton; Welford Arm, a one-and-a-half miles long narrow canal, from the Main Canal to Welford Basin; Market Harborough Arm, a five-and-a-half miles long canal, from the junction for Leicester on the main Line to Market Harborough.

The Leicester Main Line of the Grand Union Canal runs nearly seventy-eight miles from Norton Junction to Langley Mill. Locks on the Norton to Foxton section are narrow, and from Market Harborough to Langley Mill are broad.

The Grand Union Canal has junctions with several other canals and rivers, including the Thames at Brentford and Limehouse, and the Lee via the old Hertford Union Canal. Other junctions are with the Oxford Canal at Braunston and Napton; the Stratford-upon-Avon Canal at Kingswood junction; the Birmingham Canal Navigation at Birmingham; the River Trent at Trent Junction, and the River Nene at Northampton.

Grand Western Canal:

a narrow canal from Loudwell to Tiverton in Devon. Length: 10½ miles. Locks: None. Authority: Devon County Council.

Long abandoned and unused for many years, this canal is still pleasant for local boating.

Huddersfield Broad Canal

from Cooper Bridge, on the Calder and Hebble Navigation to Aspley Basin in Huddersfield. Length: 3¼ miles. Locks: 9. Authority: British Waterways Board.

Often called Sir John Ramsden's Canal, after the man

who promoted it in the 1770s, this short canal once provided a link between the Calder and Hebble Navigation and the now closed Huddersfield Narrow Canal. The Aspley Basin is a marina with good facilities. (The seventy-mile Huddersfield Narrow Canal is used by canoeists.)

Kennet And Avon Canal And Navigation:

a broad canal from the Thames at Reading, Berkshire, to Hanham Lock on the Bristol Avon. Length: 86½ miles. Locks: 105. Authority: British Waterways Board.

Once nearly derelict, this canal and river navigation has been the object of massive restoration and reconstruction work for many years. The navigation falls into three parts: the rivers Kennet and Avon at either end, and the Kennet and Avon Canal between the two. When this canal is finally re-opened it will provide a waterway through some of England's most beautiful countryside. The canal is particularly interesting because of its splendid engineering, the flight of twenty-nine locks and attendant side ponds at Devizes being one of the wonders of the whole canal system.

Various sections of it are already open to boats, and canoes can manage most of it with some porterage. The main navigable sections are from Reading (the Thames junction) to above Towney Lock, about ten miles; from Newbury to Little Bedwyn Lock; from Crofton Top Lock to Devizes Top Lock; and from the Dundas aqueduct to the Avon river in Bath.

Lancaster Canal (map 10):

a broad canal from Preston to Tewitfield in Lancashire. Length: 42½ miles. Locks: None on main canal; 7 on Glasson branch (7 miles to River Lune and sea). Authority: British Waterways Board.

Once running as far as Kendal in the Lake District, this canal is now isolated from the main system, and can only be entered from the sea via the Glasson Dock branch, or

The Chirk aqueduct, with the railway viaduct next to it, on the Llangollen Canal

you could trail your boat to Preston. The scenery round this canal is very beautiful, with splendid views over Morecambe Bay. It also has some magnificent aqueducts.

Leeds And Liverpool Canal (map 10):

a broad canal running from Leeds at the junction with the Aire and Calder Navigation to Liverpool, at the junction with the River Mersey. Length: 127 miles. Locks: 91. Authority: British Waterways Board.

This is a queen among canals – if canals are feminine! Most of the countryside through which it passes is magnificent, rising high over the Pennines, 487 feet above sea level at its highest point, so that its engineering is also spectacular. The staircase locks include the famous Bingley Five-rise, there is a great flight of locks at Wigan, many swing bridges, and the 60-foot high Burnley Embankment to take you sailing over that town's rooftops.

Two points should be taken into account if you are planning a cruise on this canal. Some of the paddle-gear is unusual and requires a very large windlass to operate. The gear is also chained in places and a special Waterways Board key is needed; hire companies can tell you about it, or one can be obtained from the Waterways Board's Area or section offices. The other point is that locks between Leeds and Wigan are only 62 feet long and therefore cannot be used by full-length narrow boats.

There are branches off the canal to Rufford (seven-and-a-quarter miles, with eight locks); Leigh (seven-and-a-half miles, two locks); Stanley Dock (one and a quarter miles, four locks) and Springs (half a mile, no locks).

Llangollen Canal (map 6):

a narrow canal, from the Shropshire Union Canal at Hurleston, near Nantwich to Llantysilio, near Llangollen in North Wales. Length: 46 miles. Locks: 21. Authority: British Waterways Board.

133

A branch of the Shropshire Union, the Llangollen is just about the most popular of all canals, and can become quite crowded in summer, especially around the locks, tunnels and aqueducts, the most spectacular of which are the famous Chirck and Pontcysyllte aqueducts. The latter was engineered by Thomas Telford, is made of wrought iron, is 1007 feet long and has been standing 126 feet above the fast-flowing River Dee since 1805.

Both the locks and the several lifting bridges are worked by boat crews, so that the Llangollen is really less than ideal for the first-time boatman. Much of the scenery on the first part of the canal is not outstandingly attractive, either, while at the really lovely part, towards Llangollen, the water is too shallow for boats with a deeper draught. The current is often such that the canal here seems more like a small river. Llangollen itself is a delightful town.

Macclesfield Canal (map 6):

a narrow canal, from the junction with the Peak Forest Canal at Marple to the junction with the Trent and Mersey Canal at Hall Green. Length: 26¼ miles. Locks: 13 (including the stop lock at Hall Green). Authority: British Waterways Board.

Following what is one of the loveliest routes of any English canal, the Macclesfield is part of the Cheshire Ring. Much of it is elevated, so the holidaymaker has the sensation of sailing above the countryside, which, since it is on the edge of the Peak District, can be spectacular. The canal passes several quietly attractive towns, and a handful of stately homes, and can offer the canaller a flight of twelve locks at Bosley, several swing bridges, some snake bridges and aqueducts taking the canal over river and ravine.

Manchester Ship Canal (map 10):

a broad commercial navigation from the River Mersey at Eastham Locks to Manchester. Length: 36 miles. Locks:

5. Authority: The Manchester Ships Canal Co. Port of Manchester, Dock Office, Trafford Road, Manchester, M5 2XB. Tel: 061 872 2411.

This great waterway is part of the busy port of Manchester and, for obvious reasons, hire-cruisers are not allowed to navigate it. Any pleasure craft wishing to do so must get the permission of the Ship Canal authorities, who will provide them with maps of a safe through-route.

The Ship Canal is of such historic interest, as well as being alive with commercial activity today, that it is well worth taking one of the day trips which operate on the canal so that you can view it at close quarters.

Monmouthshire And Brecon Canal (map 3):

a canal from Brecon in south Wales to the Pontymoyle junction with the Monmouthshire Canal. Length: 33¼ miles. Locks: 6. Authority: British Waterways Board.

This canal's name is something of a misnomer. The old Monmouthshire Canal is for the most part no longer navigable, though it is being tidied up, and it is only the Brecon and Abergavenny Canal section which may be used. This, though, should be sufficient for anyone as the Brecon is possibly the most breathtakingly lovely of any of the English and Welsh canals. It is a contour canal, winding round the hills at the edge of the Usk valley in the Brecon Beacons National Park. High on the canal's list of unforgettable pleasures must be the views from the stone aqueduct which takes it over the Usk.

Many of the hire-boats available on the canal, which is completely cut off from the rest of the canal system, are cruisers, as locks will take a boat with an 8ft 6in beam.

New Junction Canal (map 9):

a broad canal, from Pollington, 7 miles west of Goole, to Bramwith. Length: 5½ miles. Locks: 1. Authority: British Waterways Board.

Interesting because it was dug as late as 1905, this canal

135

links the Aire and Calder Canal with the Sheffield and South Yorkshire.

Oxford Canal (map 2):

a narrow canal, from the junction with the River Thames above Osney Lock to the junction with the Coventry Canal at Hawkesbury, near Coventry. Length: 77 miles. Locks: 43. Authority: British Waterways Board.

A popular canal with summer holidaymakers, this was one of James Brindley's earliest, which accounts for the twisting and bending route which is one of its attractions. The canal begins in the heart of Oxford and passes through very pretty countryside and attractive villages. Numerous wooden lift-up bridges and other old buildings add to its undoubted charm.

There is a junction with the Grand Union Canal at Napton, and from here to Braunston the two canals share the same waterway.

Peak Forest Canal (map 10):

a narrow canal, from the junction with the Ashton Canal at Dukinfield, Ashton-under-Lyne to Buxworth Basin and Whaley Bridge. Length: 14¾ miles (plus ½ mile to Whaley Bridge). Locks: 16. Authority: British Waterways Board.

A canal of great contrasts and considerable interest. The contrasts lie in the scenery it passes: urban Manchester, buildings which are relics of the Industrial Revolution, and a stretch of really beautiful countryside of the kind extolled by poets, between Whaley Bridge and Marple. The interest lies in its construction. There are two tunnels, a great stone aqueduct over the Goyt river, and a glorious staircase of sixteen locks at Marple. The canal forms part of the Cheshire Ring.

There is a junction with the Macclesfield Canal at Marple.

136

Pocklington Canal:

a broad canal from Canal Head near Pocklington to the River Derwent at Cottingworth, Yorkshire. Length: 9½ miles. Locks: 9. Authority: British Waterways Board.

Another canal whose re-opening resulted from much hard work by volunteers and the British Waterways Board, the Pocklington is at present cut off from the main canal system as the Derwent itself needs much work to restore cruiser navigation at this point. The canal is navigable for over four miles from the river; above this, it is only suitable for light craft such as kayaks.

Regent's Canal:

a broad canal, a branch of the Grand Union, from Warwick Avenue, Paddington, to the River Thames at Limehouse. Length: 8⅝ miles. Locks: 13. Authority: British Waterways Board.

A splendid urban canal, the Regent's Canal dates from the refurbishing of London which John Nash carried out for the Prince Regent, hence Regent Street, Regent's Park and this canal. A cruise along it gives some splendid and unexpected views of London from new angles, and takes in a wide range of urban styles as it passes from the late Georgian elegance of Paddington, Regent's Park and Little Venice through Camden, St Pancras, Islington, Shoreditch, Bethnal Green and Stepney to the busy Thames at Limehouse.

A short branch canal, the Hertford Canal, connects the Regent's Canal from Bethnal Green via Hackney with the Lee Navigation and the River Lee.

Rochdale Canal:

a broad canal running entirely through urban Manchester from the junction with the Ashton Canal at Ducie Street to the junction with the Bridgewater Canal at Castlefield.

Length: 2 miles. Locks: 9. Authority: Rochdale Canal Company, 75 Dale Street, Manchester M1 2HG. Tel: 061 236 2456.

Considering its length, this must be about the most expensive piece of cruising on the canal system. It is an essential part of the Cheshire Ring, but because it is privately owned, a separate navigation licence is required; the BWB licence is not reciprocal. In 1981 the single (one-way) licence fee is £12.00 if you get it in advance, £14.00 if you 'pay at the door'. There is no cheap-rate return fare.

Sheffield And South Yorkshire Canal (map 9):

a broad canal from the junction with the River Trent at Keadby to Sheffield. Length: 43 miles. Locks: 29. Authority: British Waterways Board.

This is a commercial waterway, with government approval recently granted for improvements which will allow vessels carrying substantial loads to use the canal. It makes its way mostly through industrial areas and is probably not the ideal canal for holidaymakers, though its commercial use means that some interesting craft, not seen on purely leisure canals, may be encountered, while there is much to interest the student of industry and industrial archeology.

The canal links up with the Aire and Calder Navigation via the New Junction Canal.

Maximum length for craft using the Sheffield and South Yorkshire is 61 ft 6 in.

Shropshire Union Canal (map 6):

a mainly narrow canal, from the Autherley junction with the Staffordshire and Worcester Canal to the junction with the Manchester Ship Canal at Ellesmere Port. Length: 66½ miles. Locks: 46. Authority: British Waterways Board.

138

Another very popular cruising canal, known to most canal enthusiasts as the 'Shroppie', the Shropshire Union was engineered by the great Thomas Telford, and his cuttings, embankments and aqueducts are still features of the canal today. Among the towns and villages on its route, Chester is outstanding.

The north-east section of the canal, between Nantwich and Ellesmere Port, has broad-beam locks.

The canal has one branch, the ten mile Middlewich branch, and a junction with the Llangollen Canal at Hurleston, near Nantwich.

Staffordshire and Worcestershire Canal (map 5):

a narrow canal, from Stourport on the River Severn to Great Haywood on the Trent and Mersey Canal. Length:46 miles. Locks: 43. Authority: British Waterways Board.

An interesting canal for the enthusiast, the Staffs and Worcs can offer a fine collection of locks, bridges and aqueducts, two tunnels and junctions with three other waterways, the Stourbridge Canal, the Birmingham Canal Navigations and the Shropshire Union Canal. In fact, James Brindley built the Staffs and Worcs to link the Birmingham Canal Navigations to the Shropshire Union Canal, and much of his original engineering can still be traced along it. The canal passes through some lovely countryside, and Stourport is a most interesting town, with its origins in the early days of the canal system. The canal is popular with holidaymakers and can be very busy in summer.

Stourbridge Canal (map 5):

a narrow canal, from Stourton Junction on the Staffordshire and Worcestershire Canal to Black Delph on the Dudley Canal, part of the Birmingham Canal Navigations. Length: 5¼ miles. Locks: 20. Authority: British Waterways Board.

Here is something to test your crew's efficiency: the 'Stourbridge Sixteen', a flight of locks restored by canal society volunteers and the British Waterways Board, and now one of the more famous pieces of engineering on the canal system.

Stratford-upon-Avon Canal (map 5):

a narrow canal from the junction with the Worcester and Birmingham Canal at King's Norton to the River Avon at Stratford-upon-Avon. Length: 25½ miles. Locks: 56. Authority: Northern section (King's Norton to Kingswood) – British Waterways Board; Southern section King's Norton to Stratford-upon-Avon – The National Trust, the Canal Office, Lapworth, Solihull, Warwickshire. Tel: Lapworth 3370.

A quietly pleasant canal winding through typical English countryside down to the great tourist centre of Stratford-upon-Avon. This is another canal where much voluntary labour was needed to restore it to full use. The work was carried out on the southern section, which is owned by the National Trust. Everyone using this section must pay a navigation fee, which at present is £11.00 for the whole stretch. The BWB licence cannot be used on the stretch in lieu of the fee, nor can the National Trust membership card.

Trent and Mersey Canal (map 7):

a mainly narrow canal from Derwent Mouth on the Trent to Preston Brook on the Bridgewater Canal. Length: 93½ miles. Locks: 76. Authority: British Waterways Board.

One of the earliest canals in Britain, the Trent and Mersey was planned and largely built by James Brindley, though he died before it was completed. He was supported in the building by Josiah Wedgwood, who saw its potential for transporting his pottery. Engineering of particular interest on the canal includes the 2919 yards Harecastle Tunnel and the Anderton Lift, which lifts boats from the

River Weaver level to the Trent and Mersey. Much of the canal's route lies through industrial areas, but there is sufficient green and pleasant countryside to make it an attractive as well as an interesting waterway.

The Trent and Mersey has a branch, the seventeen mile Caldon Canal, running from it at Etruria to Froghall and Leek.

River Witham Navigation (map 8):

a broad waterway, from the junction with the Fossdyke Canal at High Bridge, Lincoln, to Boston, Lincolnshire. Length: 36½ miles. Locks: 3. Authority: British Waterways Board.

This navigation and the Fossdyke Canal are often treated as one waterway, as together they form a forty-eight mile navigation across the Fens. The River Witham Navigation is very much a Fens' waterway, with the hill on which Lincoln Cathedral stands being one of the few highpoints on the flat land. Boats can enter the Witham Navigation Drain from the River Witham via a side lock at Anton's Gowt. It is also possible to enter the Wash via the Grand Sluice at Boston, which marks the end of the non-tidal river. It is not an easy passage and novice boatmen should avoid it.

Worcester and Birmingham Canal (map 5):

a narrow canal, from the River Severn at Worcester to Worcester Bar, near the centre of Birmingham. Length: 30 miles. Locks: 58. Authority: British Waterways Board.

This is a good canal for a holiday cruise. It passes through some attractive countryside, with many interesting places to visit, including Worcester and Droitwich. The locks will keep you on your toes: of the fifty-eight, thirty come in one flight, the famous Tardebigge flight, the top lock of which is 453 feet above sea level. There are also five tunnels on the route, and it would be wise to check with the British Waterways Board's Canalphone service

141

The famous flight of thirty locks at Tardebigge on the Worcester and Birmingham Canal

that they are all open before you start out on this canal.

The Thames

The Thames is far from being the longest river in Europe, it is only 209 miles long from its source near Cirencester in Gloucester to its mouth, but from the point of view of the holidaymaker it must be the most attractive. The Royal River, as it is also called, has had a long history of pleasure cruising, and can offer today's cruising holiday-maker or the person simply 'messing about in boats' some of the best amenities and facilities in the country. The Thames after all, was the setting for *The Wind in the Willows*, and there is still a rather splendid house called Toad Hall on the road from Marlow to Henley. There are many attractive riverside villages and pleasant towns, any number of pubs with gardens stretching to the water's edge, dozens of restaurants and fine hotels. Off the main river various navigable tributaries and other rivers, including the Wey, Lee and Medway, provide more waterways full of interest.

There are also, of course, many boatyards offering the boating fraternity excellent services. Some, like Salter Brothers of Folly Bridge, Oxford, established in 1858, have existed since early in Victoria's reign. At least one, R.J. Turk and Sons of Kingston, 'Waterman to H.M. the Queen', can trace its beginnings to the time of George III.

Many of these boatyards build their own fleets of well-appointed cruisers for sale or hire, and operate as chandlers on a large scale. Many also offer a complete hire service, including pump-out stations, rubbish disposal areas, refuelling services, and even toilet facilities including showers for their customers. Many of them use the main booking agencies (except Educational Services) for their bookings but there is also a number of well-established independent operators on the Thames.

As on the Broads, Thames hire-cruisers are maintained

143

to a good standard of safety and comfort. Many, though not all, operators are members of the Thames Hire Cruiser Association, a trade association which has laid down standards for the craft owned by its members. The Association also operates a rescue service whereby anyone who does have trouble with his craft can get help from the nearest Association member, rather than having to wait for his own boatyard to come to his assistance. Apart from the agency brochures, the best source for the names and addresses of hire companies on the river is *The Thames Book*, the Link House publication which I referred to in Chapter 2.

Some Thames History

The Thames has been an important highway in England for centuries, at least since Roman times, though navigation was not easy in its upper reaches, with its many shallows. A special shallow draught barge, the West Country Barge, was developed for the upper Thames, and it is only during the past ten years or so that commercial barge traffic has virtually come to an end on the Thames.

Goods and passengers were carried by boat from the centre of London to the towns of Berkshire and Buckinghamshire from the early seventeenth century, while in medieval times such riverside abbeys as Bisham and Hurley sent their grain tithes by water to Westminster. The tithe barn at Hurley, just a short walk from Hurley lock, was recently restored as a beautiful and elegant private house complete with medieval dove cote.

The building of the canal network in the second half of the eighteenth century brought more trade to the Thames, where the canal narrow boats became known as 'monkey boats'. The completion of the Oxford Canal in 1790, for instance, provided a route for coal from the Midlands down to the south, and the system of canals which came to be called the Grand Union, linked the Thames from Brentford with Birmingham and Leicester.

Downriver of London, the Thames presented a different face. Here it linked great ports which, up to World War II, were among the most important in the world, handling the cargoes of a vast empire. This was the Thames of the great London docks, of Greenwich and Tilbury, of Samuel Pepys and Charles Dickens.

It is, however, the history of the Thames as a royal river which is most likely to interest present-day holidaymakers. There was a time when the royal barge was as important a form of royal transport as the royal coach, and the State Barges, rich with gold leaf and velvet hangings, which now rest in the National Maritime Museum at Greenwich, were once regular sights on the river. Royal residences form the links in a rich historical chain stretching much of the length of the river, and offering the visitor many hours of interest and enjoyment.

Everyone can name the great palaces: Windsor Castle towering above the Thames and the town at its feet; the great mass of Cardinal Wolsey's Hampton Court Palace with its elegant Wren additions; the remains of Richmond Palace set back from the river on Richmond Green; the Dutch-style prettiness of Kew Palace and its charming garden just showing over the high wall before Kew Bridge; the brooding presence of the Tower of London, whose blood-stained past seems still to linger, even on the sunniest day; and elegant Greenwich set behind stone porticoes and green lawns where the Thames air is already beginning to smell more of sea than river.

There are also many other royal links with the Thames, and just searching them all out can form a pleasant holiday occupation. You might visit Oxford, for instance, where royal links abound. King Alfred is credited with having founded University College, Henry VIII certainly established Christ Church, and the city became Charles I's capital during the Civil War.

Cliveden, on the north bank of the Thames between Cookham and Maidenhead, was once the home of the Duke of Buckingham, and was rented by George III's father, Frederick Prince of Wales, who lived there in

145

great style from 1739. In the Rustic Theatre in the grounds, Frederick heard the first performance of Dr Arne's music for the *Masque of Alfred*, including *Rule Britannia!* Frederick also lived for a time at Marlow Place, a fine early Georgian house now occupied by business companies off Marlow's High Street. Pleasure craft can moor at both Cliveden and Marlow to visit these places.

The Thames Today: The Non-tidal River (map 1)

The Thames as a leisure river falls neatly into two sections: the upper non-tidal Thames above Teddington lock, and the tidal Thames from Richmond to the sea. An obelisk 293 yards downstream from Teddington lock marks the boundary.

The 124-miles-long non-tidal Thames is the real holiday section, and it is here the hire-boat operators are situated. Most hire craft are not permitted to navigate below Teddington Lock, but as the part of the river from Teddington up to Lechlade, the limit of navigation for craft of any size, can show some of the loveliest country-side in southern England, as well as many interesting towns and villages, this is no hardship.

It is a good waterway for novice sailors, too, as the current is not swift, except after times of heavy rainfall. Most of the river is broad with plenty of room for boats to pass each other, and the forty-four broad beam locks are all manned.

The care of the non-tidal Thames is the responsibility of the Thames Conservancy Division of the Thames Water Authority, and it does its work wonderfully well. The upper Thames must be just about the most immaculate river in Europe, as an inspection of any of the lock keepers' houses and gardens would demonstrate.

The Thames is a public highway under a charter granted under Magna Carta, and all pleasure craft operating on the non-tidal Thames must be registered. Powered craft must also be licenced, and the licence is issued free of charge to the boat's registered owner. It must be clearly displayed so that lock keepers and other river staff may see it easily (so don't drape towels and the like over it).

Hire-craft are, of course, registered and licenced by their owner operators. Owners of private craft should apply for details to the Thames Conservancy Division of the Thames Water Authority, Nugent House, Vastern Road, Reading, RG1 8DB. Telephone number for craft registration is Reading 593300. (The Conservancy's general telephone number is Reading 593333.)

The charge for registration varies according to the length and beam of the craft and on whether it is powered or not. Short-period registration is available for bona fide visiting craft normally used on other waterways, including the tidal Thames. There are restricted summer services for issuing short-term registrations at Molesey and Osney locks.

The Thames Conservancy also supplies free of charge to the owner of each registered craft, the *Launch Digest* which contains a summary of the rules and regulations which all river users should be familiar with before they set out on the Thames. The *Launch Digest* should be kept aboard all hire craft.

Important bye-laws which must be carefully observed, cover:

Speed: powered craft must not navigate at high speeds on the Thames. No boat should move at more than eight miles an hour and in most cases a safe speed will be considerably less than this. Pleasure craft skippers should remember that the Thames is more frequented than other inland waterways by small craft such as punts and small rowing boats, skiffs, canoes and kayaks. A heavy wash from a large boat could overturn any of these light craft, with disastrous consequences. A heavy wash may also wash away the river bank and cause other damage. *Watch your wash* is a catch phrase to be engraved on the hearts of all river users.

Rubbish and sewage: the Thames is a major source of domestic water for London, and it is absolutely forbidden

147

to empty sewage or throw rubbish of any kind into the water. The Water Authority has provided plenty of disposal points for rubbish and pump-out facilities for sewage. Lists of both of these may be found in the *Launch Digest* and in the hire-boat companies' literature. Petrol and oil can also pollute the water and so must never be emptied into the river.

Navigation: it is an offence to navigate any craft on the river without proper care and caution, or to navigate it at a speed or in a manner which might endanger the safety of other people and craft, or to damage the river banks. The horn signals for navigation, which were set out in Chapter 5 apply as much to the Thames as to other waterways. A navigation hazard which could give inexperienced launch drivers a nasty fright is a fleet of racing yachts, which could suddenly be encountered on a reach. The best advice here is to slow down and keep out of their way. If you cannot manoeuvre out of the way, the correct horn signal to give is four short blasts: 'I am unable to manoeuvre'.

The Thames Water Authority has a uniform system of marker buoys to indicate shoals and other hazards on the river's main navigation route. When proceeding upstream, the markers are:

Red Can: leave on your port (left) hand when going upstream.

Green triangle: leave on your starboard (right) hand when going upstream.

Red and white sphere: pass either side.

Two black spheres: isolated danger, pass all round.

When proceeding downstream, the buoys are left on the opposite hand.

Safely Through The Thames Locks

All of the non-tidal Thames' forty-four locks are worked by lock keepers, who come on duty at 9 am every day and work through until about dusk: 5 pm in winter and 7.30

pm (8 pm on bank holidays) in summer. The lock keepers' hours of duty are always posted beside the locks.

The broad Thames locks will take half a dozen or so average-size cruisers at one time, but there are still often queues of boats waiting to lock through on busy summer weekends. The Conservancy has provided lay-bys for waiting boats. These are either piles and walings off shore, suitable for larger craft, or bankside moorings.

Once your boat is in the lock, you should always act on any instruction from the lock keeper. He may direct you to one side of the lock, or tell you to move up, for instance. He is not trying to be difficult, but is fitting in as many boats as possible at one time, something of which he has a great deal more experience than you. Never moor beyond the vertical white line painted on the lock side; this will ensure that your stern does not get caught on the lock sill, which you won't be able to see below the surface of the water.

So that you can hear any instructions from the lock keeper, you should switch off your engine, radio, cassette player etc.

Other points to remember about passing through locks: do not fend off with hands or feet; make fast head and stern; keep your mooring lines fairly taut, but be ready to adjust them as the water rises or falls; do not open fuel tanks or strike matches.

It sometimes happens that a lock keeper working alone has time off for a meal break, but there is always a notice displayed to warn you. When the lock keeper is not on duty, the public may work the lock themselves, though it must be emphasised that they do so at their own risk.

Thames locks are not difficult to work, and you do not have to carry a lock key on your boat to operate them. Most of the locks have been mechanized and the handle works hydraulically. On non-mechanical locks the handle is permanently attached. Lock paddles on Thames locks are called sluices, and they must be opened slowly to empty or fill the locks, but not before you have ensured that the lock gates are properly closed.

You should always leave locks emptying or empty, with the gate shut, as in many cases there is a public right of way over the lock gates.

Waterways Off The Non-tidal Thames

From the Thames you may enter four other river navigations.

The *River Wey*, which may be entered from the Thames at Weybridge is a very pretty and not over-frequented navigation down to Guildford and Godalming. Back in the early nineteenth century it was going to be part of a great navigation all the way from the Thames down to Portsmouth, via the Basingstoke Canal, but the scheme was never completed. Today the National Trust owns and maintains the river, and boats must be registered with them. Address: the National Trust, Dapdune Lea, Wharf Road, Guildford, Surrey. Tel: Guildford 61389.

The *River Kennet*, leading into the Kennet and Avon Canal Navigation seventy yards below High Bridge in Reading, comes within Thames Water jurisdiction, so you need no extra registration or licence to explore it from the Thames. It is a short waterway with one lock, Blakes Lock, which will take craft with an 18 ft 11 in beam. The recommended maximum draught for vessels on the river is 3 ft 3 in (1 metre).

The *Kennet and Avon Navigation* was once passable all the way to Bristol, but now has only a nine mile stretch from Reading suitable for cruisers. Other stretches are being gradually repaired and restored. This is a British Waterways Board navigation, and their licence must be carried.

The Oxford Canal, a narrow canal which can be entered from the Thames via the Sheepwash Channel above Osney Bridge or via Dukes Cut, above Kings Lock. This is also a British Waterways Board navigation, and gives access to the English and Welsh canals system. A BWB licence is needed.

The tidal Thames is controlled by the Port of London Authority, whose jurisdiction extends from just below Teddington Lock to the sea, a distance of about ninety miles. Within its compass are three great docks systems, the Isle of Dogs (India and Milwall Docks), the Royal Docks in Woolwich Reach, and Tilbury Docks in Essex. Thus, the tidal Thames is a busy and important commercial waterway, and should be avoided by novice boatmen. Even those with experience should treat the tidal Thames with great care, for tides can be very strong, and the waters of the estuary very choppy.

There are a large number of passenger boat services operating on the tidal Thames, many of them from points in central London, including Westminster Bridge, Charing Cross Bridge and Tower Pier. They go downstream as far as Greenwich and upstream as far as Hampton Court Palace, and can provide a pleasant and relaxed way of seeing London and her historic river from a new angle.

Pleasure craft whose skippers know what they are doing, and can calculate tide tables, can, of course, navigate freely on the Thames, and do not have to pay any tolls. The Port of London publishes two booklets which everyone should have: *Pleasure Craft Users' Guide to the Tidal Thames* and the *Tide Table*. Both are obtainable from: The Port of London External Affairs Dept., World Trade Centre, East Smithfield, London , E1.

Other advice and information for navigating the tidal Thames can be obtained from Port of London piers, the harbour service launches which patrol the river, or from the three section officers:

Upper section (Teddington to Tower Bridge) – The Assistant Harbour Master, Toll House, Kew. Tel: 01 940 8288.

Middle section (Tower Bridge to Crayfordness) – Assistant Harbour Master, Gallions Entrance, London E16. Tel: 01 476 5005.

Lower section (Crayfordness to the sea) – Assistant
Harbour Master, Thames Navigation Service Building,
Gravesend. Tel: 0474 68111.

The Leisure Thames

Angling: as on other rivers, you will need a rod licence if
you are over sixteen years of age. With a licence, parts of
the Thames can be fished free, but other sections will also
require permits or day tickets. These sections are usually
well signposted. Rod licences can be obtained from tackle
shops and some hire boat operators, or direct from The
Fisheries Officer, Thames Water Authority, Thames
Conservancy Division, Nugent House, Vastern Road,
Reading, RG1 8DB. The Thames Conservancy can also
supply a leaflet on reservoir angling.

Walking: the Thames towpath runs almost unhindered
from Putney to Lechlade, though at various points it
crosses from one bank to the other. At one time, ferry
boats operated at these crossings, but no longer, so
walkers and ramblers can't always use the public footpath
right of way which follows the towpath for most of its
route. This is a problem the Ramblers Association has
been trying to sort out for some time and maybe one day
people will be able to walk the length of the river. In the
meantime, walkers will find the Ramblers' Association
fact sheets of great value. They may be obtained from the
Association, 1-5 Wandsworth Road, London, SW8 2LJ.

Tourist sights and sites: the two major tourist boards for the
Thames area are:

The Thames and Chilterns Tourist Board, P.O. Box 10,
8 The Market Place, Abingdon, Oxfordshire. Tel: Abingdon 22711.

The London Tourist Board, 26 Grosvenor Gardens,
London SW1W 0DU. Tel: 01 730 0791.

Each of these can send you booklets and pamphlets of
things to see and do. They also have lists of the local
tourist information centres, most of which provide local

rather than regional information.

The Severn And Avon Rivers

Flowing through areas that the Tourist Board describes as England at its most beautiful, these rivers are possibly the most attractive in the country. Both wind through lovely valleys; the Avon through the Vale of Evesham and the Severn through the Severn Valley, revealing the glories of the Cotswolds and Shakespeare country. Charming old towns and villages together with access to the rest of the canal system, add to the attractions for the holidaymaker.

The Severn is a British Waterways Board Navigation, and its five immaculately kept broad-beam locks all have lock-keepers, usually available from 6 am to 7.15 pm, to help you. The river is navigable for forty-two miles from the junction with the Staffordshire and Worcestershire Canal at Stourport to Gloucester Docks, and although it is possible to get down to Sharpness on the river, the Gloucester and Sharpness Canal is a safer alternative route. The bigger towns on the river have good facilities for boats, with moorings and slipways, fuel, chandlery and provisions available.

Cruising on the broad, sometimes swift-flowing river, is generally quiet and peaceful, with little commercial traffic to be met these days. Watch out for weirs; unlike those on the Thames they are not protected, though they are well sign-posted.

That the Warwickshire Avon is now navigable after a century of neglect and decay, is almost entirely due to the efforts of armies of volunteers, plus the inspiration of C.D. Barwell and David Hutchings. Mr Barwell bought a controlling interest in the Lower Avon in the late 1940s and, with the help of the Inland Waterways Association, set up a charitable trust to restore and develop the river. David Hutchings, who led the restoration work on the Stratford-upon-Avon Canal, was also the prime mover behind the gigantic task of restoring the Upper Avon. Today, the Avon Ring, of which the River Avon Navigation is a major section, is one of the most popular cruising sections of the inland waterways system.

The navigation links up with the Stratford-upon-Avon Canal in Stratford near the Memorial Theatre. Ambitious plans are afoot to carry on with the work of extending the Avon's navigability to Warwick where it would link up with the Grand Union Canal.

There are seventeen locks to be negotiated along the Avon, which is navigable for forty-two miles from its junction with the Severn at Tewkesbury to Stratford. It is administered by two authorities:

Upper Avon (Stratford-upon-Avon to Evesham): The Upper Avon Navigation Trust Ltd, 10 Guild Street, Stratford-upon-Avon, Warwicks.

Lower Avon (Evesham to Tewkesbury): The Lower Avon Navigation Trust Ltd, Gable End, The Holloway, Pershore, Worcs.

There is a scale of registration charges for craft using the Avon, and owners of private boats should contact the two authorities for details. Fees depend on the size of the craft, whether it is powered and where it will be used. You can obtain a combined 'Avon Ring' registration which allows you to use the Upper and Lower Avon and the Stratford-upon-Avon canal with one permit. Hire-boat operators can arrange this for you, of course.

There are many hire-boat operators on these two rivers, offering wide-beam cruisers and the traditional narrow boats sleeping up to ten or twelve people, which will allow you to get from the rivers in to the canal system. The Severn and Avon features as an area in the brochures of the big agencies – Blakes, Boat Enquiries, the Central Booking Agency and Hoseasons – as well, so you will have plenty of choice for a hire-boat holiday in this lovely part of England.

Other River Systems In England

Apart from the popular rivers we have already described,

England has several other rivers which can provide delightful cruising holidays. They are less well-known, but also less crowded and boat-hire agencies, especially Hoseasons, can offer holiday boats on several of them.

The River Wey, which runs off the non-tidal Thames at Weybridge, has already been described in the Thames section (see p. 143), but down river at Limehouse there are two more rivers off the Thames: the Rivers *Lee* and *Stort*. The lower Lee finds its way into the Thames at Limehouse. Navigable for twenty-seven-and-a-half miles to Hertford, the River Lee has twenty-one broad-beam locks along its route. The River Stort runs thirteen-and-three-quarter miles from its junction with the Lee at Hoddesdon to Bishop's Stortford and has fifteen locks. Both are British Waterways Board navigations, and very popular with anglers as well.

At its Thames end, the Lee is an industrial waterway, but once through Enfield the commercial traffic dwindles, the waterway takes on a more rural aspect and offers very pleasant boating. The Stort is a charming, winding river with the atmosphere of a country canal, unexpected in a navigation so close to London and commuter Essex. Both rivers have boat-hire firms operating on their routes which can offer moorings and other facilities, and these are likely to improve considerably along both rivers in the coming years now that the Lee Valley Park is getting into its stride as a multi-activity, planned leisure area.

The *Medway*, in the heart of Kent, is another southern river with plenty to offer the holidaymaker. Navigable for forty-two miles from Sheerness on the Thames Estuary to Tonbridge, the Medway provides quiet leisurely cruising through the 'Garden of England', with apple orchards, hop fields and oast houses much in evidence.

There are ten locks to be negotiated on the river, which is tidal as far up as Allington Lock, at Maidstone. The locks are worked by boats' crews, but the lift bridge at Yalding is operated by Southern Waterway Authority staff. The locks require a special key and passes, which hire-boat operators provide, but which private boat owners must obtain for themselves. The river authorities to contact for these and for fishing licences are:

Sheerness to Maidstone: Medway Ports Authority, High Street, Rochester, Kent, ME 1PZ. Tel: Medway 403731/5.

Maidstone to Tonbridge: Southern Water Authority, Town Lock, Medway Wharf Road, Tonbridge, Kent. Tel: Tonbridge 4466.

The Medway is now featured in the Hoseasons brochure, with completely new boats available for hire from 1980 in the Southern Water Authority's division of the river. The hire-boat operators avoid the tidal Medway which can, particularly at the Thames Estuary, become dangerous in squally weather.

Yorkshire and the North can provide three fine rivers to discover by boat: the *Ouse, Trent* and *Derwent*, which form an inter-connecting system of waterways providing junctions with several canals.

The Ouse is probably the least attractive of the three, though this is not to deny the pleasantness of the cruising on stretches of it, particularly on the non-tidal section above Naburn Locks. Along this section is York, with its magnificent Minster, medieval streets, railway museum and other attractions. Navigation below Naburn can be made difficult by a fast flowing tide, creating strong currents. The River Ure, a short (seventeen-and-a-half miles) and pleasant waterway, joins the Ouse at Swale Nab; near its head of navigation is Ripon Cathedral.

The lovely, little-used Derwent joins the Ouse at Barmby-on-the-Marsh and is navigable for nineteen miles to Stamford Bridge, though smaller craft have another sixteen miles of navigation as far as Malton, a stretch which is particularly memorable for the magnificence of its scenery. Craft must be small, however, as they have to be portaged round four disused locks.

The third of these northern rivers, the Trent, is navigable for nearly ninety-five miles between Shardlow, where there is a junction with the Trent and Mersey Canal, and Trent Falls, a junction with both the Yorkshire Ouse and the Humber. The Trent was once a busy waterway, but commercial craft are not much in evidence these days. The river provides a fine, wide course for pleasure craft, though it can become very strong when in flood, and should be avoided at such times. Towns of interest along the Trent include Nottingham and Newark, both of which are on the non-tidal section of the river (the river is tidal for fifty-two miles below Cromwell Lock, five miles downriver from Newark) where cruising is at its most agreeable. Hire-craft firms operate at several boat-yards and marinas on the river, and facilities for boats are good.

Coastal Sailing In Britain

Boating off-shore is not a wise activity for novices. You must know about tides and be able to read charts, cope with a compass and understand channel marking systems (buoys). You should be able to read the weather, too, so that you can see a squall coming in plenty of time to make ready to meet it.

So, if you really like the idea of do-it-yourself sailing and cruising at sea, rather than on inland waterways, and it can certainly be a very exciting and exhilarating pastime, the first thing to do is to stop being a novice! I have already referred to the sailing tuition which the two big agencies, Blakes and Hoseasons, can offer their customers. Hoseasons can also arrange a complete sailing holiday at a water sports centre in Scotland, where good accommodation is provided while you learn about sailing, taking either an informal beginner's course or instruction leading to a Royal Yacht Association Certificate. Other sailing schools, where accommodation is also provided, are included in the Thames/Magnum publication *Outdoor and Activity Holidays in Britain*.

Once the basics have been mastered, your next step might be to try flotilla sailing, where you and four or five friends or family can hire a boat to join a small flotilla whose mother ship is commanded by a very experienced sailor. Hoseasons offer these holidays from Inverary in Scotland and off the south coast of England out of the Hamble.

There are hire-boat operators throughout Britain who will charter yachts or motor cruisers to experienced sailors for coastal cruising. Others can provide charter yachts and cruisers with a skipper and full-board accommodation or skippered craft where you do your own catering. A wide-ranging Information Sheet on Coastal Cruising and Yacht Charter in Britain is available from the British Tourist Authority, 64 St James Street, London SW1A 1NF. Tel: 01 629 9191. The booklet lists the charter operators and gives details of the kinds of craft they have available, the waters they cruise in, and their charges. It also indicates the kind of experience the hirers will expect you to have.

The Highlands and Islands Development Board, Bridge House, 27 Bank Street, Inverness, IV1 1QR has a booklet, *Yachting, Boating and Cruising*, which lists the yacht and cruiser charter firms, both skippered and self-drive, which operate off the Scottish coasts and islands.

Once introduced to the pleasures of costal sailing, you may want to join a club (which will have its own craft you could use), join the crew of a private boat, or even buy your own craft. You should also consider joining the Royal Yachting Association, the national organisation which co-ordinates the work of individual clubs while looking after the interests of sailing and power-boating in general. The Association's main address is 70 Brompton Road, London, SW7. Tel: 01 589 4666. Their Training Division is at Victoria Way, Woking, Surrey, GU21 1EQ, which is the address to write to for a list of the teaching establishments they recognise and for advice on other aspects of learning to sail.

Waterways In Scotland

Scotland is a glorious country for a waterway holiday. The

scenery can be breathtakingly beautiful, with a rugged grandeur not found in the more soft and gentle south, both sea and inland lochs offering peace, solitude and superb fishing un-matched anywhere else in Britain.

There are waterways in Scotland suitable for all kinds of boating holiday, from leisurely cruising on the Caledonian Canal, and exhilarating sailing among the western isles, to canoeing in more sheltered waters such as Glencoe, the Spey Valley and Loch Ness. Facilities for the boat-owner and boating holidaymaker are good, offering chandlers, repair yards, mooring places with shops, and other facilities readily available.

The Scottish Highlands and Islands Development Board's useful booklet, *Yachting, Boating and Cruising* gives names and addresses of all boatyards, repair yards, chandlers etc., in their area, plus detailed lists of yacht and cruiser hire and charter operators.

Blakes and Hoseasons include a wide choice of Scottish self-drive hire-boat holidays in their brochures. Loch Ness and the Caledonian Canal have been established as inland hire-boat holiday centres for many years and Loch Lomond has recently been added to the list. From boatyards based at Oban and Onich, both agencies also offer more experienced sailors holiday cruising among the sea lochs of the western coast, and, further south at Inverary, on upper Loch Fyne, Rothesay on the Isle of Bute, the Firth of Clyde and the Kintyre Peninsula.

Waterway holidays in Scotland can also include short cruises among the islands. There are three companies which organise three-, four- or five-night cruises during the summer (May to September):

Caledonian MacBrayne Ltd, the Ferry Terminal, Gourock, PAI9 1QP, tel: 0475 33755, offers cruises from Oban to the islands of Iona, Coll, Tiree and Colonsay, including accommodation in two-berth cabins and all main meals.

P & O Ferries Orkney and Shetland Services, P.O. Box 5, Jamieson's Quay, Aberdeen, AB9 8DL, tel: Aberdeen 572615, offers cruises from Aberdeen to the Orkney and

The ruins of Castle Urquart on Loch Ness on the Caledonian Canal waterway in Scotland

Shetland islands.

West Highland Cruises, Windaves, Kirn, Dunoon, Argyll, PA23 8DT, tel: Dunoon 3167, whose cruises depart from Oban and include the islands of the inner and outer Hebrides as well as a five-night cruise of the Caledonian Canal. The Company's vessel is a twin screw diesel yacht, with accommodation for twelve passengers.

The Scottish Canals (map 11)

Scotland has four main canals, the Caledonian Canal, the Edinburgh and Glasgow Union Canal, the Crinan Canal and The Forth and Clyde Canal. All come under the jurisdiction of the British Waterways Board who, with the help of the Scottish Inland Waterways Association, has done much valuable restoration work in recent years, though there remains much to be done if all four canals are to become valued leisure amenities.

The main Scottish office of the British Waterways Board is at Old Basin Works, Applecross Street, Glasgow, G4 9SP. Tel: 041 332 6936.

The *Caledonian Canal* is unique in Britain in that its construction in the 1820s was government-financed. It was built by Thomas Telford and links the east coast of Scotland with the west via four canal sections (totalling twenty-one-and-a-half miles), and three fresh-water lochs (Ness, Oich and Lochy). There are twenty-nine broad-beam locks to be negotiated, though there are lock keepers to help. The total length of the waterway is sixty-one-and-a-half miles and it takes about one and a half days to traverse, partly because the 6mph speed limit is strictly enforced, and partly because locks are closed before 8am and after 5pm on Mondays to Saturdays. (They are closed all day on Sunday, unless you can persuade the BWB in advance that they should be opened for you.) The Board's Caledonian Canal Office is at Clachnaharry, Inverness, IV3 6RA. Tel: Inverness 33140. The BWB licence does not cover the toll charges which also have to be paid.

The Caledonian Canal could provide you with an unforgettable cruising holiday. The scenery in Scotland's Great Glen is superb, with pine and heather covered hills sweeping down into the great lochs, and charming grey-stone towns including Inverness, Fort Augustus and Fort William waiting to welcome you. If you leave your boat moored, there is Ben Nevis or Glen Moriston to be explored, nature reserves and trails to be walked, and historic houses and castles to be visited.

Loch Ness is the largest of the three lochs, twenty-three miles long, about one mile wide and, at 700 ft, is deeper than the North Sea. Its waters can look dark and cold, even on the sunniest day, so it is no wonder that the legend of the Monster lives on. It is a legend which the forbidding ruins of Castle Urquhart on the shores of Loch Ness do nothing to dispel.

While traversing Loch Oich, pause a while to look at the ruins of Invergarry Castle. Bonnie Prince Charlie stayed at this home of the Macdonnells before and after the Battle of Culloden in 1746, which is why Butcher Cumberland's men destroyed it. The castle stands in the grounds of the delightful Glengarry Castle Hotel, and if you want a night away from your boat, this is the place to spend it.

The *Edinburgh and Glasgow Union Canal* runs thirty-one-and-a-half miles from Edinburgh to Falkirk, and, although it is blocked in several places by roads, it has some attractive cruising and canoeing sections. It is used by boat trips and some private craft are moored on it.

The *Crinan Canal* cuts across the Mull of Kintyre from Ardrishaig to Crinan on the Sound of Jura, and is nine miles long with fifteen locks. Fishing boats and sea-going vessels use the canal to avoid the long passage round the Mull of Kintyre, and a cruise on it offers peace and attractive scenery.

The *Forth and Clyde Canal* runs thirty-five miles from Grangemouth on the Firth of Forth to Bowling on the Firth of Clyde. It was once an important link in the Scottish canal system, but decayed badly after it was closed in 1962. The Scottish Inland Waterways Association and the British Waterways Board have been doing much to restore sections of it and it is hoped eventually to re-open the whole canal to leisure use. At present there are two short sections usable by smaller craft and canoes.

Tourists's Scotland

The Scottish Tourist Board publishes an excellent list of booklets, pamphlets, maps and other material of use to the visitor to Scotland. Their address is: The Scottish Tourist Board, 23 Ravelston Terrace, Edinburgh, EH4 3EU. Tel: 031 332 2433.

Tourism in the western highlands and islands is the responsibility of the Highlands and Islands Development Board, Bridge House, 27 Bank Street, Inverness, IV1 1QR. Tel: Inverness 34171.

For information about local happenings in the Loch Ness area, contact the Inverness, Loch Ness and Nairn Tourist Organisation, Information Centre, 23 Church Street, Inverness. Tel: Inverness 34353.

Waterways In Ireland

Holidays on the inland waterways of Northern Ireland and Eire are easily arranged through local operators, or through Blakes and Hoseasons, both of whom offer a good range of Irish waterway holidays in their brochures.

In Northern Ireland, the major holiday cruising area is the 300 square miles of Upper and Lower Lough Erne and the Erne river. The river and the lakes, which contain hundreds of delightful, mostly uninhabited little islands, form a quiet, miraculously uncrowded waterway. There is superb coarse fishing all year round, and game fishing from March to October. (You would need a licence, but this can be obtained locally without difficulty.)

The countryside of the Erne is very beautiful, with well-forested hills, pleasant towns and villages, and numerous castles and stately homes to be visited. Swimming from sandy bays and coves, water-skiing, and dinghy-sailing are all available.

The Erne waterway is navigable for over fifty miles from Belturbet in County Cavan to Belleek, home of the famous pottery. The main navigation channels are all clearly marked, using a system of posts topped with semi-circular plates painted orange, with a green stripe along the side on which you must pass.

Boats for holiday hire are mostly broad-beam cruisers, fully equipped with gas cookers, showers and modern toilets. Many also have central heating.

In Eire, the River Shannon, the Grand Canal and the River Barrow are the main waterways for hire-boat holidays, cutting a route through the centre of Ireland where some of its loveliest countryside may be found.

There are about a dozen operators on these waterways, with 500 well-equipped cabin cruisers and narrow boats on the Grand Canal) on offer. Blakes and Hoseasons both feature the waterways in their catalogues, or you can obtain a detailed information sheet, *Cruising on inland waterways*, from the Irish Tourist Board (see below for address), which lists names and addresses of operators and notes the size of boat, facilities on board and rates per week applicable to each operator. Most self-drive hire-craft include a dinghy, charts and binoculars in the hire fee, and radio and TV are available. The Irish Tourist Board will have inspected and approved all the boats.

You do not need a licence for Irish waterways, but hirers must be over twenty-one and the boat's controls must be understood by at least two people on board. Tuition or familiarisation courses are available when you collect your boat.

As well as self-drive craft, river barges offering one or two weeks' skippered cruises on the Shannon for groups of eight to ten people are also available. The cruises can be either fully inclusive or self-catering. A company offering these cruises is Weaver Boats Ltd, Carrick-on-

Shannon, Co. Leitrim, Eire. Tel: Carrick-on-Shannon 204.

The *River Shannon* is navigable for 140 miles from Lough Key at its northern end to Killaloe. It is non-tidal for 128 miles, and has only six locks, all of which are supervised by lock keepers from 9 am to dusk. There is a small locking up fee. Navigation channels are marked with buoys: keep black markers on your starboard (right) side when going upstream and the red markers on your port (left) side. The system is reversed when going downstream. Red poles or flags indicate hazards.

There is a whole string of attractive loughs on the Shannon, two of which, Ree and Derg, are large enough to be more like inland seas, while the countryside on either side changes from rich parkland and rugged mountains to gentle pastures and well-wooded banks. Picturesque bridges, pretty villages, ancient ruins and modern restaurants provide contrasts and attractions on this lovely waterway.

The Shannon is famous for its fishing; bream, perch, pike and rudd all being in good supply. You do not need a licence for coarse fishing, and there is no close season, though the fishing is at its best in spring and early summer. Most boatyards hire out rods and lines, and will also arrange the licence you do need if you want to fish for salmon, the season for which is from 1 March to 30 September.

The *Grand Canal* connects the Shannon with Dublin, and offers eighty miles of canal cruising, with only twenty-four locks on the route. At Robertstown, the Barrow Line of the Canal heads down to Athy and the River Barrow, which is navigable as far south as St Mullins. This canal and river waterway offers 150 miles of quiet and beautiful cruising, where you will not have to queue at the locks and may not see another boat all day.

Canoeing

Canoeing is developing fast in Eire, which is hardly

surprising considering the number of rivers ideal for canoeing which the country can offer. The main canoe-touring rivers are the Liffey, Barrow, Nore, Boyne and Slaney; the lakelands of the Midlands or Kerry are perfect for novice canoeists.

The Irish Canoe Union has a Touring Officer with assistants in the four provinces, who can give the canoe tourist much helpful advice and assistance, and provide river sheets for the main canoe rivers. Write to the Touring Officer, Irish Canoe Union, c/o Cospoir – The National Sports Council, Floor 11, Hawkins House, Dublin 2.

The Tourist In Ireland

It is always a good idea to get plenty of tourist literature well before your holiday starts to help you plan your time. The Irish tourist boards all produce a wealth of helpful material. Addresses are:

- *Northern Ireland:*
   Northern Ireland Tourist Board, River House, 48 High Street, Belfast, BT1 2DS. Tel: Belfast 31221/46609.
Eire:
   Irish Tourist Board – Bord Failte, Baggot Street Bridge, Dublin 2. Tel: Dublin 765 871. Or, Irish Tourist Board, 150 New Bond Street, London, W1Y 0AQ. Tel: 01 493 3201.

CHAPTER 7

Added Enjoyments

People who have never been on a waterway holiday often think of it as being a rather slow affair, with the boat chugging along, doing no more than fifteen miles a day, and everyone sitting about quietly on deck. 'What do you do all day?' is a question often asked. In fact, there is so much one can do, keeping the boat shipshape, preparing meals and the like, as well as stopping to visit places en route, that every day can pass by in a whirl of activity.

It is undeniable, though, that children may find a waterway holiday a bit difficult, cooped up in a confined space for long periods. The wise parent will have planned in advance various activities which may start out as just something 'to keep the children occupied', but which may well turn into an absorbing interest which will give hours of added enjoyment and help make the holiday memorable.

Natural History

A waterway holiday is ideal for learning more than you would have thought possible about nature and wildlife. You are travelling slowly enough to see in detail things which, in a car, pass by in a blur. And you have plenty of opportunities just to stop, look and listen – the best way of finding out about nature.

It is a good idea to take with you a selection of field guides or inexpensive plant, bird, animal and insect identification guides. These are invaluable for helping you put a name to the plants and creatures of riverbank

167

and waterway which you will encounter in profusion. More important, they are the foundation stones on which your own personal collection can be based.

When walking in the countryside you will find feathers, fur and, perhaps, small bones of birds and mammals which, once correctly identified and annotated, can form the basis of a very good collection. Generally, though, a collection based on the wildlife you may see on holiday is more likely to be a log book or journal illustrated with photographs or drawings, something which will jog the memory when you take it out long after your holiday is over.

The same points apply to a plant collection, though with these you have a much better opportunity to collect the objects themselves. Bear in mind that many wild flowers in Britain are protected species, and it is illegal to uproot them. You should never take out clumps of plants from river banks, either; you could be destroying the habitats of animals or birds as well as doing irreparable damage to the river bank. A small cutting, carefully taken, will not damage the parent plant and is all that you need. The cuttings can be pressed between the pages of a heavy book, or in a small flower press, which will not take up much room in your holiday baggage.

There are some plants you may encounter on holiday which no flower press will be large enough to take. Water weeds like those found on the River Nene are so large that their leaves resemble cabbage or rhubarb, and their stalks are thick enough to wind themselves round the propellers of your boat. If you want a reminder of these, you will have to use your camera or pencil.

A waterway holiday is very much a holiday in the country too, so you should be aware of the main points of the Country Code, evolved by the Countryside Commission to let everyone enjoy the countryside now, while preserving it intact for future generations. The Code's ten points are:

Guard against all risk of fire.

Fasten all gates.

A canal camping boat with distinctive decoration moored in the Coventry Basin

Keep dogs under proper control.
Keep to the paths across farmland.
Avoid damaging fences, hedges and walls.
Leave no litter.
Safeguard water supplies.
Protect wildlife, wild plants and trees.
Go carefully on country roads.
Respect the life of the countryside.

Buildings And Engineering

A waterway holiday is all the more enjoyable if you get really involved in the nuts and bolts of it. Before you go, try to read a few books about canals and canal history, or about the formation and geology of rivers. Knowing something of how locks are constructed, or why canals were cut to follow certain routes, or even that bridges over canals are numbered and that the number plates are different shapes and sizes, all helps you to become personally involved.

This is particularly true of children, and it is a fact which parents can put to good use on a boating holiday. Give a child a notebook and pencil, and he can become the waterway equivalent of a train spotter, writing down the name, type and owner of every boat he sees. Or he can note the wording on notices at locks and bridges; many of these are very old and refer to weights for horse-drawn vehicles and so on.

The camera gives everyone the means to preserve a record of waterway engineering and buildings. Photographing all the lock keepers' cottages on the Thames would be an interesting project – colourful, too, because Thames lock keepers seem able to grow bigger and brighter marigolds in their riverside gardens than anyone else. Photographic records of locks, bridges, waterside warehouses and offices, tunnels and aqueducts, maintenance yards and marinas can have a social and historical value as well as giving personal satisfaction.

Collecting the ephemera – the printed paper throwaways – which any holiday generates is an easy way of creating an album of holiday memories. It could also be the beginning of a worthwhile hobby, for paper ephemera has become collectable, like postage stamps and postcards. There is an Ephemera Society in London, which publishes a journal of well-researched articles by members, holds regular meetings, and arranges sales and auctions of ephemera. The Society's address is 5 Fitzroy Square, London, W1.

A collection of waterway ephemera can be started very easily; simply keep the brochures, maps and handbooks sent to you by the hire-boat operator or booking agency. Add to these the booking confirmation forms, invoices and receipts you will get when paying for the holiday plus your travel tickets, train or bus time tables, river tide tables, toll tickets.

Of course, you could specialise. Take beer bottle labels, for instance. Any canal addict will tell you that one of the great joys of narrow boating is that first glorious, thirst-quenching pint at some canal-side pub at the end of a long day's cruising.

If the beer comes in a can, keep the can; there have been books written about beer can collecting, too, so you are into a hobby with world-wide ramifications. For the ephemera collector, however, the beer must come in bottles because it is the label he is interested in. Even in these days of mass-produced and mass-marketed beers, there are still many local brews to be discovered and enjoyed, each one of them with its own label. If the collector is really serious, he will keep a note of where and when he bought the beer, and even if he enjoyed it, so that when he comes to mounting his collection in an album it will have a complete story to tell.

At the top end of the ephemera collecting market are items from the past, particularly ones with a rarity value or with connections with a well-known person or historical event. The sort of things you would be searching for in connection with the waterways would include old trade cards with charming eighteenth-century or Victorian engravings on them; notices of auctions of craft and chandlery; freight and toll receipts; notices announcing stoppages or the closure of a canal; brochures and timetables; menu cards from cruise ships . . . The list is lengthy and the resulting collection delightful.

Folly Bridge.

CHAPTER 8

Clubs and Societies

This is a chapter of names and addresses, and may not be of great interest to readers until they have enjoyed their first waterway holiday. Then, I hope, their interest in our waterways will have been kindled sufficiently for them to want to know more about about their history, help in their restoration and preservation, and take part in the activities which surround them. The clubs and societies listed here are a selection from the large number to be found in all parts of the country. Many others are listed in the British Waterways Board's *Waterway User's Companion*.

General Associations

Inland Waterways Association: 114 Regent's Park Road, London NW1 8UQ. Tel: 01 586 2510.

The IWA is the national organisation for everyone interested in Britain's waterways, and is concerned with the restoration and development of the waterway system so that it can be put to full recreational and commercial use. The Association has seven regions, each of which has numerous branches, so it within reach of most people in the country. Branches hold regular meetings, lectures, outings and rallies, and can also find plenty of work for people who want to help actively in the restoration of canals and navigations.

Since it was founded in 1946, the IWA has played a major part in restoring the country's once derelict waterway system to good use. It has raised armies of workers to clear canals, has fought numerous impressive legal battles, and has published several reports which have aroused national interest.

One of its most successful publicity and fund-raising efforts has been its national rally, to which boats and boat people come from all over the country. The 1981 National Rally is being held at the British Waterways Board yard at Dock Street, Leeds, on 15 and 16 August.

Scottish Inland Waterways Association: c/o 25 India Street, Edinburgh, EH3 6HE.

This association was formed in 1971 to promote the conservation, development and use of all inland waterways in Scotland, but at present it is concentrating its energies on the Scottish canals. It is campaigning for the increased recreational and commercial use of the Caledonian and Crinan canals, and is working towards the restoration of the Forth and Clyde and Union canals.

Narrow Boat Trust: Hon. membership sec: P. Gibbons, 44 Main Street, Middleton, Derby, DE4 4LU.

The aims of the trust, which was set up in 1971, are to restore and preserve canal narrow boats and barges of all descriptions, whether horse-drawn or powered; to exhibit them for the benefit of the public; and to promote the use of such boats in commercial canal carrying. The trust owns two all-steel motor boats built in the 1930s and is working towards the preservation of a butty boat to work with one of them.

Local Organisations

East Anglian Waterways Association: Wych House, St Ives, Cambridgeshire, PE17 4BT.

This association is a registered charity, concerned with the protection and preservation of inland and tidal waterways in East Anglia. It sees its main task as ensuring that nothing is done on East Anglian waterways which might destroy their beauty and amenities or deprive individuals of the ability to use them to the full. It has done much valuable work in supporting waterway users

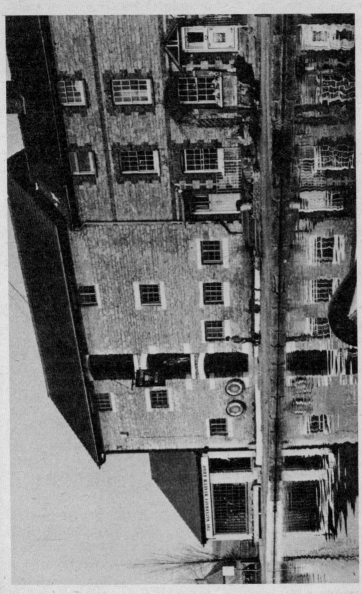

The Waterways Museum at Stoke Bruerne on the Grand Union Canal

with such problems as power lines over rivers and canals, closed navigation, low trees etc.

The association has its own representative on the Water Recreation Sub-Committee of the Eastern Sports Council. Its work has been invaluable to the future of the waterways of East Anglia.

River Thames Society: Gresham House, Twickenham Road, Feltham, Middlesex, TW13 6HA. Tel: 01 894 5811.

A society whose main aim is to ensure that the amenities of the Thames are preserved for all to enjoy. The society works to encourage an active interest in the history, present and future affairs of the river, to preserve and extend its present amenities, and to assist in the development of art, science, sport and recreation associated with the river.

The society also operates a Thames Information Centre from its Feltham office which offers a service to all users of the river, for pleasure or business.

There are more than thirty societies and associations all over the country, with aims similar to those of the East Anglian Waterways Association and the River Thames Society, some of them connected with large waterways, some with small, local ones. The Link House publication *The Canals Book* lists them all, and you may well find one near you that you would like to join.

Museums

There are several museums devoted either entirely or in part to waterways, their history and operation, which are well worth a visit. Foremost among them is The Waterways Museum, Stoke Bruerne, near Towcester, Northants. Tel: Northampton 862229.

This museum, run by the British Waterways Board, lies alongside the Grand Union Canal, and contains exhibits covering two centuries of canal history, including a full-size reconstruction of a butty boat cabin fitted out and decorated in traditional style. The museum is open daily in summer from 10 am to 6 pm, and from 10 am to 4pm in winter (except Mondays).

Other museums with interesting waterway collections include The Canal Exhibition Centre, The Wharf, Llangollen, Wales; and The Black Country Museum Trust, Tipton Road, Dudley, West Midlands (at the approach to the Dudley Canal Tunnel).

Colliers Unloading.

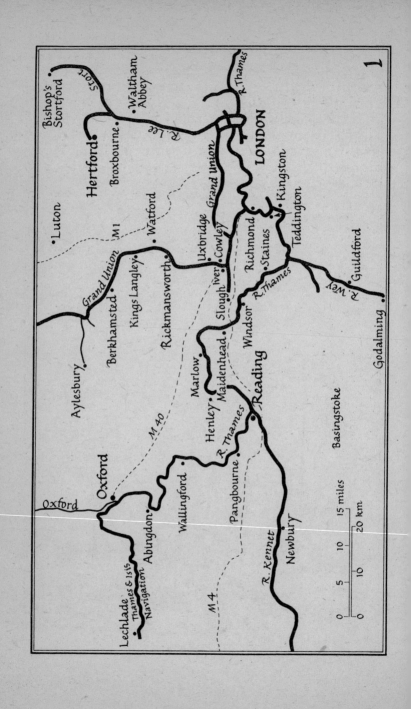

1

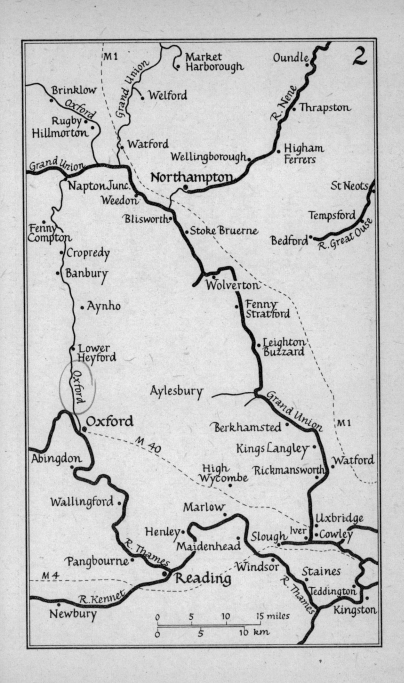

2

M1

Grand Union

Market Harborough

Oundle

Brinklow

Oxford

Welford

R. Nene

Thrapston

Rugby
Hillmorton

Grand Union

Watford

Wellingborough

Higham Ferrers

Northampton

St Neots

Napton Junc.

Weedon

Tempsford

Fenny Compton

Blisworth

Stoke Bruerne

Bedford

R. Great Ouse

Cropredy

Banbury

Wolverton

Aynho

Fenny Stratford

Lower Heyford

Oxford

Leighton Buzzard

Aylesbury

Grand Union

M1

Oxford

Berkhamsted

Kings Langley

Watford

Abingdon

M 40

High Wycombe

Rickmansworth

Wallingford

Marlow

Uxbridge

Henley

Maidenhead

Slough

Iver

Cowley

R. Thames

Pangbourne

Windsor

Staines

M 4

Reading

R. Thames

Teddington

R. Kennet

Newbury

Kingston

| 0 | 5 | 10 | 15 miles |

| 0 | 5 | 10 km |

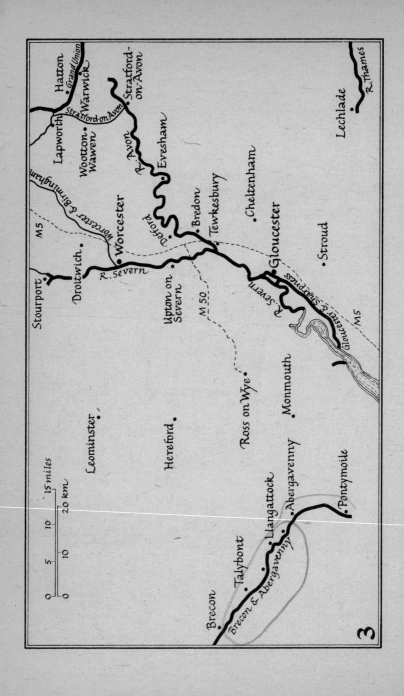

Hatton

Grand Union

Warwick

Stratford-on-Avon

Lapworth

Wootton Wawen

Stratford-on-Avon

R. Avon

Evesham

M5

Worcester & Birmingham

Droitwich

Worcester

Bredon

Tewkesbury

Cheltenham

Stourport

R. Severn

Dutford

Gloucester

Stroud

Upton on Severn

M 50

R. Severn

Gloucester & Sharpness

M5

Leominster

Hereford

Ross on Wye

Monmouth

15 miles

20 km

Brecon

Talybont

Llangattock

Abergavenny

Pontymoile

Brecon & Abergavenny

0   5   10   15 miles

0   10   20 km

R. Thames

Lechlade

3

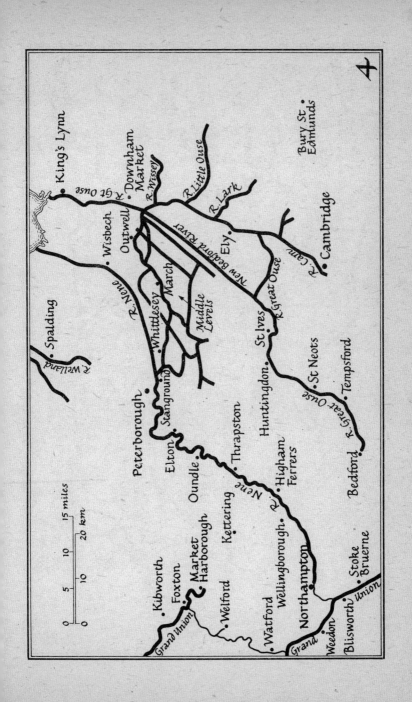

4

King's Lynn

Bury St
Edmunds

Spalding

Downham
Market

Outwell

R. Gt Ouse

R. Wissey

Wisbech

R. Little Ouse

R. Lark

R. Welland

R. Nene

New Bedford River

Ely

Whittlesey

March

Cam

R. Cam

Cambridge

Middle
Levels

R. Great Ouse

Peterborough

Stanground

St Ives

Elton

St Neots

Huntingdon

Oundle

Thrapston

Tempsford

15 miles

Kettering

Higham
Ferrers

R. Great Ouse

20 km

Nene

Wellingborough

Bedford

10

Kibworth

Welford

Watford

5

Foxton

Market
Harborough

Northampton

10

Weedon

Stoke
Bruerne

0

0

Grand Union

Grand

Blisworth

Union

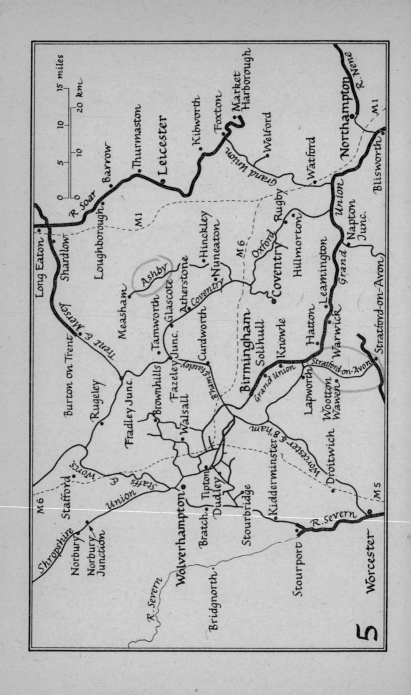

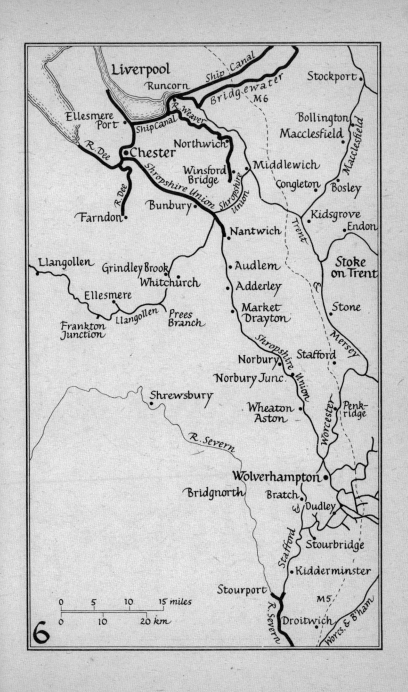

Liverpool

Runcorn

Ship Canal

Bridgewater

M6

Stockport

Ellesmere Port

Ship Canal

R. Weaver

Bollington

Macclesfield

Macclesfield

R. Dee

Chester

Northwich

Middlewich

Winsford Bridge

Shropshire Union

Shropshire Union

Congleton

Bosley

R. Dee

Bunbury

Farndon

Nantwich

Trent

Kidsgrove

Endon

Llangollen

Grindley Brook

Audlem

Stoke on Trent

Whitchurch

Adderley

Ellesmere

Frankton Junction

Llangollen

Prees Branch

Market Drayton

Stone

Shropshire Union

Norbury

Mersey

Stafford

Shrewsbury

Norbury Junc.

Wheaton Aston

Penkridge

Worcester

R. Severn

Wolverhampton

Bridgnorth

Bratch

Dudley

Stafford

Stourbridge

Kidderminster

M5

Stourport

Droitwich

R. Severn

Worcs. & B'ham

0 5 10 15 miles

0 10 20 km

6

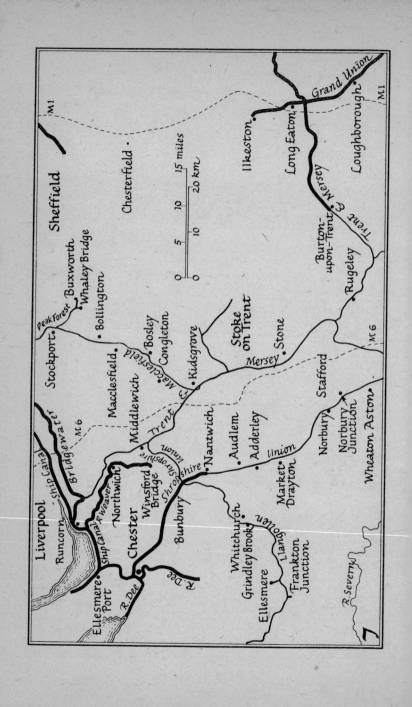

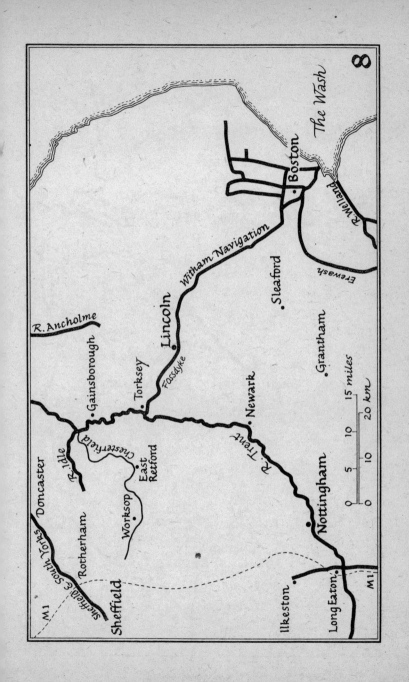

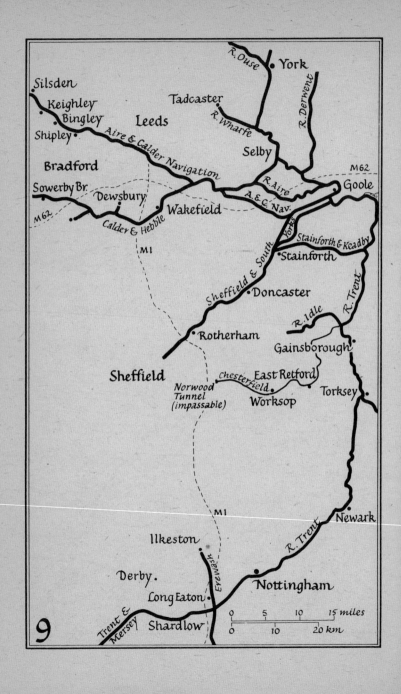

9

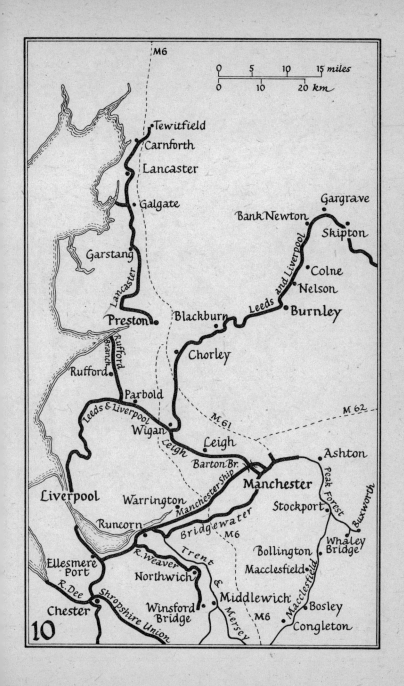

M6

15 miles
20 km

Tewitfield
Carnforth
Lancaster
Galgate
Garstang
Lancaster
Preston
Rufford Branch
Rufford
Parbold
Leeds & Liverpool
Wigan
Leigh
Leeds and Liverpool
Bank Newton
Gargrave
Skipton
Colne
Nelson
Burnley
Blackburn
Chorley

M 62

M 61
Leigh
Barton Br.
Ashton
Manchester
Peak Forest
Buxworth
Stockport
Liverpool
Warrington
Manchester Ship
Bridgewater
Runcorn
M6
Bollington
Macclesfield
Whaley Bridge
R. Weaver
Trent
Ellesmere Port
Northwich
R. Dee
Shropshire Union
Middlewich
Macclesfield
Chester
Winsford Bridge
& Mersey
M6
Bosley
Congleton

10

HEBRIDES

• Ullapool

• Inverness

Loch Ness ←

Caledonian Canal
(from Clachnaharry,
Inverness Firth to
Corpach, Loch Eil)

• Fort Augustus
Loch Oich
Loch Lochy
• Fort William

Loch Linnhe

• Oban

Loch Fyne

Forth & Clyde Canal
(from Grangemouth
to Bowling)

Crinan •

• Grangemouth

Bute
• Rothesay

• Falkirk
Glasgow ↑ • Edinburgh

Crinan Canal
(from Ardrishaig,
Loch Fyne to Crinan,
Sound of Jura

Arran

Edinburgh & Glasgow
Union Canal
(from Edinburgh to
Falkirk)

11

Pumping Out Stations

This list has been supplied by the Association of Pleasure Craft Operators. They ask that if your boat has a holding tank, please phone the boatyard in advance.

This blue and white sign shows location of stations.

	Telephone	Opening Hours
Fossdyke and Witham		
Brayford Trust Ltd., Brayford North, Lincoln, Centre of City	0522 214522	6 days 9 am–6 pm
Foxline Cruisers, Sinclairs Mill, Dogdyke, Tattershall Br. 10 miles from Boston, 21 miles from Lincoln	0526 42124	7 days 9 am–Sunset
Leeds & Liverpool Canal		
Rodley Boat Centre, Bridge 217	0532 576132	7 days
Bradford Boat Services Ltd., Apperley Bridge, Swing Bridge 214	0274 612827	Mon-Thurs 9–5. Fri & Sat am only. Closed Sun.
Appollo Carriers Ltd., Victoria St. Br. 107B, Shipley	0274 595914	7 days 9 am–5 pm
Pennine Boats of Silsden, Br. No. 191A	0535 53675	Mon-Sat 8.30 am-5 pm
Snaygill Boats Ltd., South of Br. 182	0756 5150	9am-5.30pm Closed all day Tues. Sat and Sun am.
Pennine Cruisers, Canal Basin, Spring Bench Junction	0756 2061 or 5478	7 days 8.30 am-5.30 pm.
Yorkshire Dales Hire Cruisers, Bank Newton Locks	075 678 492	Mon–Fri 9am-4.30pm
L and L Cruisers, Rawlinsons Br. No. 71	0257 480825	Mon–Fri 8.30 am-5.30 pm.

Coles Morton Marine Ltd., Mayors Boatyard, Wigan, next to BWB Yard	066 33 2226	Mon–Fri 9.30 am–4.30 pm. Sat. Noon–4.30 pm.

North East River Trent

Fiskerton Wharf, 1 mile N. Hazelford Lock	0636 830695	Mon–Sat 8.30am-4pm 'phone first
Northerner Boats Ltd., Yacht Basin, Misterton	Gainsborough 890450	Mon–Sat 9am-4.30pm 'phone first

Bridgewater Canal

Claymoore Navigation Ltd., Bet. M56 and A56 Bridges	092 86 582	7 days 9.15 am–5.45 pm 'phone first
Egerton Narrow Boats, The Boatyard, Worsley (1½ hrs from Watersmeet)	061 793 7031	Sun–Fri 9.30 am–4.30 pm 'phone first

Macclesfield & Peak Forest

Coles Morton Marine Ltd., Whaley Br. Canal Basin, Terminus Park Forest Canal	066 33 2226	Mon–Fri 9.30 am–4.30 pm Sat & Sun Noon–4.30 pm.
Dyecraft Ltd. 100 yds N. Br. 87	078 16 5700	Mon–Fri 8.30am-5pm 'phone first

Shropshire Union Canal

Holiday Makers (Marine) Ltd., Br. 119	0244 36456/7	7 days 10am-5pm
Eggbridge Hire Cruisers, Br. 119	0244 36604/ 32095	7 days 9am-5pm

Wandra Boats Ltd, Br. 104	0829 260186	Tues-Sun 9 am-7 pm
British Waterways Board, Basin adjacent to Br. 92	0270 65122	Mon-Fri 9 am-5 pm
Shropshire Union Cruisers, Norbury Junction, Br. 38	078 574 292	7 days 9 am-5 pm
Countrywide Cruisers (Brewood) Ltd., Bet. Br. 14 & 15	0902 850166	Mon-Fri 9.30am-5pm
Water Travel, Autherley Junction, Adjacent Br. 1	0902 782371	Mon-Sat 9am-5.30pm

Llangollen Canal

English Country Cruises, Br. 20	0270 780 544	Sun-Thurs 9 am-5 pm 'phone in advance'
Bridge Canal Cruisers, Br. 32	0948 2012	7 days 9 am-6 pm
Black Prince Marina Ltd., Prees Arm Br. 3	094 872 420	Sun-Fri 9am-5.30pm
Maestermyn Marine Ltd., Br. 5	069 187 424	7 days 9am-7.30pm
Anglo Welsh Narrow Boats, N. end of Pontcysyllte	0978 821749	Mon-Fri 8.30 am– 5.30 pm.

Trent & Mersey Canal

Premier Narrow Boats, Bet. Br. 209 & 210	0606 852945	7 days 9 am-6 pm
New Anderton Navigation Co. Ltd., Br. 198	0606 79642	7 days 9 am-6 pm
Clare Cruisers Ltd., Barnton Tunnel	0606 77199	7 days 9 am-5 pm
Willow Wren Kearns Ltd., Bet. Br. 169 & Lock 72	060 684 2460	Sun-Fri 9 am-6 pm

Twinram Canal Hire Boat Co. Ltd., South of Bridge 126	0782 812674	6 days Mon-Sat 9 am-5 pm
Vistra Marina, Hassel Green, Sandbach Lock 57		9am-5.30pm
Midland Luxury Cruisers, Bet. Br. 94 & 95	0785 816871	Mon-Fri 10am-4pm 'phone first
Swan Line Cruisers Ltd., Fradley Junction	0283 790332	Mon-Fri 9am-5.30pm
Jannel Cruisers Ltd., Br. 33	0283 42718	7 days 8 am-6 pm
Clayton Line Ltd., Stenson Marina	0283 703113	7 days 8am-5.30pm
Plus Pleasure Marine, Shardlow	Derby 792844	7 days 9 am-5 pm
Sherwood Canal Cruisers Ltd., 200 yds. W. of Br. 3	Derby 792066	Mon-Sat
Cruiseways Hire Co., Trent Lock, Erewash Canal	Long Eaton 4643	Mon-Sat 9 am-6 pm

Staff & Worcs.

Anglo Welsh Narrow Boats, Gt. Haywood Junction	Little Haywood 881711	Mon-Fri 9 am-5am Tel. Sat & Sun
Bijou Line, Penkridge Lock	Penkridge 2732	7 days during season 9am-12.45pm 2pm-5.45pm
Teddesley Boating Centre, Parkgate Br. No. 90	Penkridge 2437	Mon-Sat 9 am-5 pm Sun am only
Gailey Marine, Gailey Lock	0902 790612	7 days 9.30am-6pm
Gregorys Canal Cruisers, Junc. Staffs & Worc/Shrop. Union	0902 783070	Mon-Sat 9 am-6 pm Sun 9am-Noon

Dartline, York St. Lock, Stourport	Stourport 2970	7 days 9 am-1 pm 2 pm-5 pm 'phone first
Cleaver Marine Ltd., in basin top of narrow locks from Severn	029 93 77222	Mon-Fri 9 am-5 pm
Worcester & Birmingham Canal Sovereign Marine, Bet. Br. 18 & 19	0905 54474	Mon-Fri 9 am-5 pm
Water Folk Ltd., Bridge 30	09057 3889	7 days
Black Prince Narrowboats, Br. 44	0527 33437	Mon-Fri 9am-5.30pm
Alvechurch Boat Centre, Br. 60	021 4452909	Mon-Thurs 9.30 am-5.30 pm. Tel weekends
Dartline Cruisers, The Old Wharf, N. end Tardebigge Tunnel	0527 73898	7 days 9am-5.30pm
River Severn & Avon Vale of Evesham Narrow Boats, Evesham Marina, Just above Evesham Lock by Railway Br.	0386 47099	Mon-Fri 9 am-5 pm
Cleaver Marine, Upstream Evesham Lock	Evesham 45544	Mon-Fri 9 am-5 pm
Sovereign Marine, St Mary's Lane, Mill Avon at Tewkesbury	0684 292187	Mon-Fri 9 am-5 pm Must Tel.
Cleaver Marine,, Downstream Beechams Yd., before King John's Br.	0684 292981	Mon-Fri 9 am-5 pm
Sovereign Marine, Lowesmoor Basin	0684 292187	7 days Must Tel. 9 am-5 pm
Cathedral Cruisers, Diglis Basin	0905 352831	Mon-Fri 9 am-5 pm
Sovereign Marine, Upton Marina	Upton 3156	7 days Must Tel. 9 am-5 pm

Stratford upon Avon Marine, Upstream Clopton Br. by Hilton Hotel	0789 69669	Sun-Fri 8.30 am-6.30 pm

Stratford Canal

Western Cruisers Ltd., Above Lock 51	0789 69636	Sun-Fri 8am-5.30pm
Anglo Welsh Narrow Boats, Canal Wharf, Wootton Wawen (Southern)	Henly in Arden 3427	Mon-Fri 9 am-6 pm

Grand Union Canal

Olton Boat Hire, Bet. Br. 84 & 85	021 7072988	Mon-Fri 9 am-5 pm
Boats (Warwick) Br. 49	Warwick 42968	Mon-Fri 9am-5.30pm summer 9am-5pm winter Tel. Sat.
Calcutt Boats, Calcutt Top Lock	Southam 3757	7 days 9am-6.30pm
Concoform Marine, Bet. Br. 24 & 25	Weedon 40739	Tues-Fri 9 am-1 pm 2pm-5.30pm
Waterways Holidays, Stowe Hill Wharf, Br. 26	Weedon 41365	7 days 9 am-1 pm 2pm-5pm
Water Gipsy Shop, Stowe Hill Wharf	0327 40763	7 days 9 am-1 pm 2 pm-5 pm
Black Prince Narrow Boats, N. End Blisworth Tunnel	0604 858868	9am-5.30pm Closed Sat & Tues.
Willowbridge Enterprises, Br. 98	0908 73571	Mon-Fri 8.30am-6pm Sat & Sun 9am-5.30pm
Wyvern Shipping Co., Br. 114, Leighton Lock	Leighton Buzzard 2355	7 days 9am-5.30pm

194

Autrant Waterway Services, Br. 120	0525 373552	Closed Weds 9 am-5 pm
Grand Union Cruisers, Br. 190	089 54 40325	7 days 9 am-5 pm
High Line Yachting Ltd., Iver	0753 651496	Mon-Fri 10am-5pm Sun. 11am- 4pm

North Oxford & Coventry

Rugby Boatbuilders, Hillmorton Wharf	Rugby 4438	Mon-Fri 9 am-5 pm
B.W.B., Bet. Hillmorton Locks 2 & 3, Br. 70	Rugby 73149	Mon-Fri 9 am-5 pm
Rose Narrow Boats, Br. 30	Rugby 832449	Mon-Sat 9 am-6 pm Sun. 9am- 4.30pm
Club Line Cruisers, Bet. Br. 4 & 5	Coventry 58864	Sun-Fri 8 am-8 pm
Valley Cruisers, Cov. Canal Bet. Br. 39 & 40	Atherstone 2602/3016	7 days 9 am-5 pm

Ashby Canal

Ashby Narrow Boat Co., Stoke Golding, Br. 25	Hinckley 212671	Mon-Sat 9.30am-5pm

South Oxford Canal

Gordons Pleasure Cruisers, Br. 109, 300 yds. S. of Napton Junction	Southam 3644	7 days 9am-5.30pm 'phone first
Fenny Marine Ltd., Bet. Br. 136 & 137	029 577461- 2	7 days Dawn to Dusk
Cropredy Motor Cycles, The Wharf, Oxford side Cropredy Lock	029 575 386	Mon-Sat 9 am- 6 pm
Anglo Welsh Narrow Boats, Aynho Wharf, Gt. Western Arm	0869 38483	Mon-Fri 9 am-5 pm
College Cruisers, 300 yds S. Br. 242, Nr. Isis Lock	0865 54343	Mon-Sat 8 am-6 pm Sun. am only

Orchard Cruisers, Isis Lock	0865 54732	7 days 8.30am-6pm

Leicester Section & River Soar

Welton field Narrowboats Ltd., Br. No. 2	Long Buck- by 842282	Mon-Fri 9 am-5 pm Tel. ahead
Black Prince Narrow Boats, Welford Arm	085 881 519	Mon-Fri 9am-5.30pm
Hucker Marine, Br. 45	Mkt. Har- borough 880484	7 days 8.30 am- 6.30 pm
Ian Goode Narrow Boats, Br. 65	Kibworth 3034	Mon-Sat 9 am-5 pm
Foxton Boat Services, Bottom Foxton Locks	Kibworth 2285	7 days 8 am-6 pm
Anglo Welsh Narrow Boats, Main Concrete Wharf, End Mkt. Har- borough Arm	Mkt. Har- borough 67076	Mon-Fri 9 am-5 pm
Seymour Roseblade Ltd., Bet. Br. 13 & 14	0533 62194	7 days
Charnwood Marine, Bet. Br. 16 & 17. Follow signs	0533 693069	Sun-Fri 9 am-5 pm
Sileby Boats, Br. 22, Sileby Lock	Quorn 43544 Sileby 3583	7 days 9am-5pm

London Area & River Lea

Lea Valley Narrow Boat Co., Victoria Basin, 50 yds upstream of Ware Br. on Towpath side	Ware 3626	7 days 9am-5.30pm

River Wey

Guildford Boathouse, Millbrook, Guildford	Guildford 504494	7 days 9 am-6 pm
Godalming Narrow Boats, Farncombe Boat House, Below Catteshall Lock	Godalming 21306	7 days 9 am-5 pm Restricted service Sat.

Two camping craft, Plover and Kildare, make 144 feet of holiday boating

Glossary

AEGRE: a tidal wave.

AQUEDUCT: bridge which holds the water of a canal as it crosses over a road, railway line, river or valley. Probably the best known canal aqueduct is the Pontcysyllte which carries the Llangollen Canal over the Dee valley.

BACAT (Barge Aboard Catamaran): barge-carrying ship service between the Humber and the Continent.

BALANCE BEAM: wooden, iron or concrete beam which is pushed across to open or close lock gates.

BARGE: canal or river boat not less than 11 feet wide, and usually 14 feet wide.

BASIN: point where a waterway widens, either at the end of the route or as a lay-by along it. Many are now used as mooring places.

BOLLARD: metal, concrete or wood tying-up points for boats.

BUTTY BOAT: narrow boat without an engine, which is towed by a powered boat.

CLOUGH (pronounced 'clow'): northern term for lock paddle.

CONTOUR CANAL: one which curves round land contours instead of cutting across them. Most early canals were of this type.

CUT: boatman's term for a canal.

DAY BOAT: craft with no living accommodation.

DRY-WALLING: timbers used in the early days of the canals to stop erosion of the canal banks. Today, concrete piling is used.

FENDERS: objects hanging along the sides of a boat to keep it off the sides of locks, jetties etc.

FLIGHT (of locks): a series of locks each one 400 yards or less from the next. The biggest flight in England is that of thirty narrow locks at Tardebigge on the Worcester and Birmingham Canal.

GONGOOZLER: common canal term, origin unknown, for people who stand about watching happenings at locks.

GUILLOTINE LOCK: found mainly on the Fens' rivers, these are lock gates which slide up and down, rather than opening like a door.

LEGGING: working a boat through a tunnel, using the legs against roof or walls, where there is no towpath, and the engine cannot be used.

LENGTHSMAN: one who regularly patrols the canals looking for signs of erosion, slipping etc.

LIGHTER: version of the traditional compartment boat, used on the Sheffield and South Yorkshire Canal in conjunction with the BACAT system.

LOCK: a system devised to allow a boat to rise or fall from one level in a waterway to another.

LOCK KEY: *see* windlass.

MONKEY BOAT: local term for a narrow or long boat on the Thames in the London area.

NAVVIE: originally a shortened form of 'navigator'; the men who cut the canals.

PADDLE: shutter below water level on the inside of a lock gate, through which water flows to empty or fill the lock chamber.

PADDLE-BAR: bar which raises the lock gate paddles.

PAWL: catch which holds up a lock paddle once it has been raised; it engages with the cog to stop the paddle closing under its own weight.

PEN: Fenland term for lock.

POUND: a stretch of water between two locks.

PUSHER TUG: large tug designed especially for pushing large compartment boats.

QUANT: a Broad's shaft.

RACK: term in Ireland for lock gate paddle.

ROVING BRIDGE: a bridge built to transfer a towpath from one side of a canal to the other.

Shiplake lock on the Thames empty during re-construction in 1961. The 'steps' are the lock sill

SHAFT: canal term for a large boathook.

SHAFTING: poling a boat along.

SHROPPIE: the Shropshire Union Canal.

SIDE POND: pond made at the side of some locks to help conserve water. Water is allowed to flow from the lock into the side pond, rather than down the canal, allowing it to be returned to the lock.

SILL (sometimes spelt 'cill'): large bar of masonry or timber below water level on the top lock gate, which holds the gate against the weight of the water in the pound. Boats must be kept clear of this when in the lock.

SLACKER: Fenland term for a lock paddle.

SLUICE: term for lock gate paddles on Thames locks.

SNAKE BRIDGE: *see* Roving Bridge.

STAIRCASE: a number of locks following straight on one from another, without a pound in between; the top gate of one lock is the bottom gate of the next one. Staircases occur where a canal has to negotiate a very steep rise. The biggest one in Britain is the eight-lock staircase on the Caledonian Canal; the Bingley Five-Rise is a well-known one in England.

STAITHE: in the Broads, a village or parish landing stage, most of them now used as mooring places with fresh water supplies for holiday boats; in Yorkshire, a wharf.

STOP LOCK: one which prevents the water from one canal flowing into another. These were usually built where a canal belonging to one company joined the canal of another.

STOPPAGE: closure of a canal or a section of a canal for repair and maintenance work.

STRAPS: official canal term for ropes.

SUMMIT LEVEL: the highest point, or points, which a canal reaches.

TOM PUDDING: coal-carrying compartment boat. Shaped like boxes and towed in long trains by a tug, they may still be seen on such commercial waterways as the Aire and Calder Navigation.

TOWPATH: waterside track especially intended for towing craft. The first in England was built along the Severn in

1581, and tolls for its use were laid down by an Act of Parliament. Towpaths are not necessarily public right of ways.

WEIR: a dam across a river to maintain the water level.

WHERRY: the traditional sailing barge of the Norfolk rivers and coast. The *Albion*, restored by the Norfolk Wherry Trust, is moored at Horning Rectory on the Broads.

WINDING HOLE (pronounced with a short 'i' as in 'windy': a turning point on a canal for full-length narrow boats.

WINDLASS: detachable L-shaped handle essential for opening most lock gate paddles.

Acknowledgements

Many people and organisations provided information for this book. Author and publisher wish particularly to thank:

The Anglian Water Authority; Richard Woolley of the Association of Pleasure Craft Operators; Blakes Holidays; Boat Enquiries Ltd; Graham Avory and Tony Grantham of the British Waterways Board for advice and assistance and the British Waterways Board for permission to quote from the *Waterway Users' Companion*; Central Booking Agency for Inland Waterways Activities; East Anglia Tourist Board; L. A. Edwards of the East Anglia Waterways Association; Educational Cruises Ltd; Hoseasons Holidays; Imray, Laurie, Norie and Wilson for permission to quote from *Inland Waterways of Great Britain* by L. A. Edwards; John Gage of the Inland Waterways Association; the Middle Level Commissioners; Spinal Injuries Association and Willow Wren Cruisers for material about *Kingfisher*; Thames Water Authority, Thames Conservancy Division.

Illustrations reproduced by permission of British Waterways Board (pp 35, 57, 72, 78, 85, 120, 132, 142, 175), Blakes Holidays (pp 12, 21, 49, 101, 160) Educational Cruises Ltd (pp 169, 197) Peter Gough, of Shiplake Lock (p200) and Edmund Swinglehurst (p 90).

Maps, except for map 11, Scotland, which was drawn by Neil Hyslop, are reproduced by permission of Penguin Books Ltd.

Line illustrations in the text were taken from an early edition of *The Book of the Thames*, a facsimile edition of which has recently been published.

The frontispiece is a photograph by Henry Taunt, a collection of his photographs was published as *The England of Henry Taunt* by Routledge and Kegan Paul. This photograph used by permission of Oxford County Libraries.

Junction of the Cherwell and the Thames.

DISCLAIMER

Outdoor and Activity Holidays in Britain

EDMUND SWINGLEHURST

Outdoor and Activity Holidays in Britain is for the growing number of people who feel that there is more to a holiday than sitting in deckchairs and strolling along the promenade. It covers holidays for all ages and for all capabilities, including the disabled, on land, air and water:

Walking	Hang-gliding
Trekking	Ballooning
Cycling	Sailing
Rock climbing	Canoeing
Pot-holing	Water skiing
Power flying	Wind surfing
Gliding	Study holidays

The organisations which give general advice and help on all these are listed, and there is a selective list of places which offer holidays of each type. It includes details of the accommodation, and approximate prices.

Edmund Swinglehurst, who works for a major international travel company, describes what each holiday entails, suggests how to choose a suitable holiday, and even includes a list of terms used in each activity.

Outdoor and Activity Holidays in Britain is a *Wish You Were Here . . . ?* Guide, published in association with Thames Television's holiday programme.

World Without Trees

ROBERT LAMB

"This splendid book is a powerful weapon in a tough struggle to save some remnant of the world's finest vegetation." *Vole*

FACT – Every minute 50 acres of tropical rain forest are cut down.

FACT – In 20 years' time there will be no rain forests left.

FACT – In Britain each year 2,000,000 elm trees are cut down.

FACT – To a large extent, the world's oxygen balance depends on trees and forests.

A world without trees would be dull and depressing. But more importantly a world without trees would be a disaster for mankind.

In this book, Robert Lamb looks at the importance of trees in our world and considers what will happen if we continue to cut them down in large numbers. His suggestions are staggering and vital.

This is a terrifying warning — which we ignore at the risk of mankind's existence.

"A courageous and disquieting book."
Daily Express

Quotations for our Time

Dr LAURENCE PETER

Here is a stimulating and witty collection of quotations from the man who discovered the Peter Principle. The focus is on ideas rather than words and the book includes gems of wit and originality from minds ancient and modern: from Plato to Freud, from Shakespeare to Woody Allen.

ART
'A painter who has the feel of breasts and buttocks is saved.' *August Renoir*

COMPUTERS
'The computer is a moron.' *Peter Drucker*

MARRIAGE
'Marriage has many pains but celibacy has no pleasures.' *Samuel Johnson*

LIFE
'Let us endeavor so to live that when we come to die even the undertaker will be sorry.' *Mark Twain*

SINCERITY
'A little sincerity is a dangerous thing, and a great deal of it is absolutely fatal.' *Oscar Wilde*

'A compendium, full to overflowing, of the remarks that illuminate the world, usually by their wit and truth, and sometimes by their stupidity. Open it anywhere and you will laugh – or wince.' *Isaac Asimov*

More non-fiction from Magnum Books

These and other Magnum Books are available at your bookshop or newsagent. In case of difficulties orders may be sent to:

Magnum Books
Cash Sales Department
P. O. Box 11
Falmouth
Cornwall TRIO 109EN

Please send cheque or postal order, no currency, for purchase price quoted and allow the following for postage and packing:

U.K   30p for the first book plus 15p for the second book and 12p for each additional book ordered to a maximum charge of £1.29.

B.F.P.O. & Eire   30p for the first book plus 15p for the second book plus 12p per copy for the next 7 books, thereafter 6p per book.

Overseas Customers   50p for the first book plus 15p per copy for each additional book.

While every effort is made to keep prices low, it is sometimes necessary to increase prices at short notice. Magnum Books reserves the right to show new retail prices on covers which may differ from those previously advertised in the text or elsewhere.